End Of The Pier
by Danny Robins

Published by Playdead Press 2018

© Danny Robins 2018

Danny Robins has asserted his rights under the
Copyright, Design and Patents Act, 1988, to be
identified as the author of this work.

A CIP catalogue record for this book is available from
the British Library.

ISBN 978-1-910067-67-3

Caution

Playdead Press
www.playdeadpress.com

A Note From The Writer

We live in a good time for comedy. It fills our screens, stand-up clubs proliferate and Twitter has reinvigorated the art of the one-liner, sending it global. More and more though, laughter is not only something that brings us together, it is also used to divide. Trump, Brexit, Abortion, #MeToo, Black Lives Matter; we're living through an ideological civil war and what you find funny is one of the most effective ways of determining which trench you are in. Humour has always been the most subjective of art forms, but I don't think it has ever been this binary, this savagely partisan.

With *End Of The Pier*, I set out to write a drama about comedy and, more specifically, its Jekyll and Hyde nature. Laughter can be joyous, but it can also be cruel. Sharing a joke bonds us, but many of you will also know how it feels to dread being laughed at. Jokes need victims, and each generation chooses its targets and its boundaries. The mainly male and working-class stand-ups of the 70s and 80s, who packed-out Blackpool Pier, are now largely expunged from history for their prejudiced stereotypes. The 'alternative' comedians who displaced them took aim at the establishment, embodied by Thatcher. As the late 90s brought prosperity, optimism and Tony Blair (hard to believe he was once popular), satire shifted its sights from politicians to celebrities. The likes of Ali G, Mrs Merton and Chris Morris dented many reputations. During the mid-noughties, I wrote jokes for various TV comedy panel shows, never quite feeling comfortable with the casual cruelty we were expected to dole out to famous people, often simply for their looks, weight or intelligence. It made me wonder if we'd really evolved that far from the mother-in-law jokes told in smoky working men's clubs. Recently, Twitter has brought a new trend, where the joke's teller becomes its victim, the misjudged or offensive gag a comedic gun that explodes in their face.

Tastes and notions of acceptability may change, but the one constant is you, the audience; the euphoric feeling we get when you laugh, and the horrible swirling panic when you don't. I can't think of another artistic medium where success or failure is so instant and so public. Comedians will do anything to avoid the awful sound of no one laughing, and that can lead to compromising principles. There's a concept within comedy of 'punching up' or 'punching down' – do your jokes target the perceived wrongs of a dominant group, or take cheap shots at those with less power? Anyone who's done a few rounds with a punchbag knows punching down is far easier. The very fact we use the term 'punching', conveys the power comedy can have, and with that power comes responsibility.

I fell in love with jokes at an early age, delighting in their distinctive, satisfying rhythm even before I understood the punchlines. I did my first stand-up gigs in my late teens in the pubs and clubs of the North-East where I grew up, and since then I have spent my life trying to make people laugh on radio, TV and on stage. Sometimes I wonder if that's been a futile, fatuous pursuit, and then I check Twitter and see all the hatred, anger and division in the world, and think maybe it's been time well-spent. Because I still believe in the fundamentally positive nature of shared laughter. When we let our guard down and the endorphins flow, we find we have more in common than we thought. Jokes may be hijacked by bullies, but they remain the perfect riposte to them too.

Danny Robins
Writer

A Note From The Director

In *End Of The Pier* Danny quotes that old adage 'all comedy needs a victim'. Even Freud believed this to be true: his theory was that humour that didn't rely on a victim (word play, or punning for example) held only minimal possibilities for real laughs. This is a concept that I think many of us will recognise, but might not like. It holds within it a suggestion that the laughing audience is malign; following a comedian's pointing finger and throwing back their heads and laughing at some poor victimised fool. But this isn't what it feels like to laugh. It isn't what it feels like to laugh at *Frasier*, or *Dad's Army* or any number of stand-ups. So if comedy needs victims, can the audience be anything other than victimising?

We can certainly be more aware of who (or what?) the victim is. As Danny has so brilliantly evoked, comedy has moved on exponentially in even the last 5 years, let alone the 30 or so during which our character Bobby has been professionally telling jokes. In the last five years we have seen an extraordinary rise of online theory, thought and sharing about the issues at the heart of this play: race, what it means to be a person of colour in the west, what it means to be white in the west, what white privilege really means: power, who has it, how do they get it, how do they use it and how it shapes lives. What this means in all areas of our lives is still being understood, but for comedy it means that it is no longer acceptable to attack people with less power than you. There are jokes that now cannot be made without severe consequences: consequences that are manifested by a different audience, a much larger, more powerful online audience.

So what is the function of an audience? We are surrounded by an audience all the time. At home: (if we don't live alone) at work, (almost certainly) online (all the time). Even as we walk down the street we will be captured by multiple unseen CCTV cameras. For an online generation an audience is at the heart of our lives. Bobby and Michael define success by audience numbers – four million or twenty million. Online celebrities are now 'influencers'. Our 'audience' influences everything we do.

For some, this is bemoaned. Headlines decrying that 'snowflakes are killing comedy' are surprisingly common: making everything 'vanilla', ironing out humour to avoid offence, leaving no room for human error. For some this is hailed: a new era of responsibility, of openness, of clarity. Whichever side of that fence you might fall on, it cannot be denied: even as part of an audience, you always have an audience yourself.

So what does this mean for an audience here in this theatre? What does this mean for you and me? As a theatre-maker, the audience is my bellwether: my guide. The whole production changes as soon as we have an audience. Previews allow the cast and me to feel how the show works: where does it creak and leak air? Where is it tight and dynamic? What do we need to shorten or where can we hold a moment? We can't do this without an audience.

For a play like this, you, our audience, are paramount. This play asks what an audience is, and what the responsibility is of that audience. It draws close to issues that are by their very nature offensive in the extreme. It asks you to understand what we are trying to expose and what we are trying to espouse, if anything. It asks you to steer us: with your laughter – the ultimate, fastest indication of approval.

Hannah Price
Director

End Of The Pier

By Danny Robins

The World Premiere took place at Park Theatre, London on 11 July 2018 with the following team:

Cast (In Order of Appearance)

Michael	**Blake Harrison**
Bobby	**Les Dennis**
Jenna	**Tala Gouveia**
Mohammed	**Nitin Ganatra**

Creative Team

Director	**Hannah Price**
Designer	**James Turner**
Lighting Designer	**Sally Ferguson**
Sound Designer	**Ella Wahlström**
Assistant Director	**Denzel Westley-Sanderson**

Production Team

Producer	**Rachael Williams**
Production Manager	**Ben Krebs**
Company Stage Manager	**Jess Gow**
Assistant Stage Manager	**Jessica Cooper**
Script Consultant	**Kurt Barling**
Stand Up Comedy Coach	**André Vincent**
Production Sound Engineer	**Andre T**
Production LX	**Phil Burke**
Costume Supervisor	**Holly Henshaw**
Set Builder	**Liam Hill**
Press & PR	**Nick Pearce & Julie Holman for Target Live**

With thanks to

Sam Alexander, Jez Bond, Lisa Makin, Jack Kelly and Bill & Elaine Strain for all their knowledge of Blackpool, Vince Peake of Springfield Sea Anglers for information about fishing on the pier, Jack Bradley, Francesca Devas, Hugo Young, Dan Tetsell, Damian McAlinney, Rose O'Sullivan, Shaun Gorringe at The Blackpool Grand, Lesley Harcourt, Michael Barrymore, Philip Wilson, Mel Hudson, Liam Shannon, Marcus Brigstocke, Shappi Khorsandi, Steve Harper, Eva, Leo & Max Robins and huge thanks to Tharik Hussain for his guidance on Bangladeshi culture.

This play is dedicated to the memory of Larrington Walker (1946-2017), one of the good guys.

CAST

Les Dennis | Bobby

Les Dennis is one of the UK's best known entertainers.

Born in Liverpool, he came to prominence as a comedian in the 1970s after honing his craft on the northern Working Men's Club circuit and turning pro after a winning set on *New Faces*. He became a stalwart of Saturday Night TV in the 80s and 90s, starring in TV comedies including *The Russ Abbot Show* and *The Les Dennis Laughter Show* performing sketches and impressions, and most famously as the host of *Family Fortunes* between 1987 and 2002 on ITV.

Theatre includes: *The Addams Family* (Music and Lyrics); *She Loves Me* (Menier Chocolate Factory); *Down The Dock Road* (Royal Court, Liverpool); *The Perfect Murder* (TPM Productions); *Spamalot* (ATG); *Hairspray* (UK Tour); *Jigsy* (Liverpool Royal Court - Best Actor LPD Arts); *When We Are Married* (West Yorkshire Playhouse); *Eurobeat* (No 1 Tour/ West End); *Certified Male* (Edinburgh Festival); *The Servant Of Two Masters* (Wales Theatre Company); *Marlon Brando's Corset* (Edinburgh Festival); *Neville's Island* (Birmingham Rep); *South Pacific* (Birmingham Symphony Orchestra); *Art* (UK Tour); *Cherished Disappointments In Love* (Soho Theatre); *Chicago* (Adelphi Theatre); *Just Between Ourselves* (Theatre Royal Bath); *Skylight* (Newbury Watermill Theatre); *Me And My Girl* (Adelphi Theatre).

Television includes: *Coronation Street, Holby City, Hotel Babylon, New Street Law, The Bill, Extras, The Quest 2, Casualty, Mersey Beat, Doctors, Brookside, Les Dennis's Liverpool, Les Dennis and Dustin Gee's Laughter Show.*

Film includes: *Wounded* (Winner Best Feature Marbella Film Festival), *Intimate Relations.*

Nitin Ganatra | Mohammed

Theatre includes: *Animal Farm* (Belgrade Theatre); *As I Lay Dying* (Young Vic); *Blessings* (B&R Prod. for The Old Red Lion); *D'yer Eat With Your Fingers?* (Stratford East Theatre); *Dice With The Devil* (Glynne Wickham Studio); *Haroun And The Sea Of Stories* (National Theatre); *I Am Not India / Kiwi* (Southwark Playhouse); *Jungle Book* (MAC); *Kootle Mountain* (Candid Café); *Les Enfants Du Paradis* (RSC); *Listening Too Fast* (International Tour); *Lucifer You...* (National Tour); *Macbeth* (Tricycle Theatre); *Oh Sweet Sita* (Tara Arts); *Parallel Lines* (Place Theatre); *Skinflicks* (Belgrade Theatre); *Testimonial* (National Tour); *The Bacchae* (Edinburgh Festival); *The Sanctuary* (National Theatre); *To The Green Fields Beyond* (Donmar Warehouse); *Touched* (Might and Man Physical Theatre co); *Turandot* (Edinburgh Festival); *Twelfth Night* (Young Vic); *Twelfth Night* (Border Crossings); *Wilder Shores of Live* (BAC); *Yobbo Nowt* (Glynne Wickham Studio).

Television includes: *Silent Witness, Crossing The Border, Cornershop Superhero, Twenty Twelve, Being April, Canterbury Tales, Casualty, EastEnders, England Expects, Extremely Dangerous, Holby City, Hounded, Indian Dreams, Jane Hall's Big Bad Bus Ride, Kumbh Mela, Me And Mrs Jones, Meet The Magoons, Mumbai Calling – Series 1, Murder In Mind, New Street Law, New Tricks, Randall & Hopkirk, Rescue Me, Revenge, Second Generation, Shadow In The North, Silent Witness, Sins, Small Potatoes, Son Of The Dragon, The Astronuts, The Bill, The Catherine Tate Christmas Special, The Grey Man, The Jury, The Real Deal, Thief Takers, This Life, Trial And Retribution, Twisted Tales "In At The Death", Welcome To Strathmore, You're Breaking Up.*

Film includes: *Hellboy: Rise Of The Blood Queen, Eaten By Lions, Bride And Prejudice, Charlie And The Chocolate*

Factory, Chess, Colour Me Kubrick, Guru In Seven, Inferno; Mad, Bad And Sad, Mistress Of Spices, Our Charley, Piccadilly Jim, Pure, Secrets And Lies, Shifty, Stag, The Drop, The Hunting Party, The Love Doctor, This Bastard Business; Truly, Madly, Deeply.

Radio Includes: *The Most Wanted Man, Midnight's Children, Bindi Business Series 2, Boyle's Law, Continuity Man, Ping Pong, BBC Radio Drama Company, The Spiritual Centre, The Places In Between, The Raj Bullworker Show, The Mahabarata, A House For Mr Biswas, Earthly Powers, Tales From Ferozsha Bag, The Guide, Grandmothers, The Minds Eye, The Sami & Winston, The Secret Parts; What Now, Now That We Are Dead, The Good Person Of Szechwan, Scoring Winds, Girlfriends, Untouchable, House Of The Sun, The Tiger, Brahmin And The Lady, Shoulders, Grease Monkeys, The Dark Horse, Accidental Death Of An Anarchist, 7 Circles Around The Fire, Year Of The Tiger.*

Tala Gouveia | Jenna

Theatre includes: *The Here and This and Now* (Southwark Playhouse); *Much Ado About Nothing* (The Faction Theatre Productions); *Talent, The Mountaintop* (New Vic Theatre); *Husbands & Sons* (National Theatre / Royal Exchange Theatre); *Muswell Hill, Romeo & Juliet* (Orange Tree Theatre); *Blue Stockings, A*  *Midsummer Night's Dream* (Shakespeare's Globe); *White Tuesday* (Arcola Theatre); *Buried Child* (Upstairs at the Gatehouse); *The Shape Of Things* (Lunatics and the Poor)

Television includes: *Cold Feet (Series 8), Holby City, Plebs, Scream Street, The Tracey Ullman Sketch Show (Series 1 & 2), Quiet Desperation, Scrotal Recall, Monks, Doctors, Shakespeare Uncovered, Trying Again, Fit, EastEnders, Deadbeats.*

Film includes: *For Love or Money, Crystal Beth, Before We Grow Old, Arrivals, Desire.*

Blake Harrison | Michael

Theatre includes: *Step 9 (of 12)* (Trafalgar Studios); *The Accidental Lives of Memories.* **Theatre whilst in training:** *Market Boy, The Good Person of Szechwan, On the Razzle, Richard III, Arms & the Man, Street of Crocodiles, Duck* (East 15).

Television includes: *A Very English Scandal, Trust Me, Drunk History, Prime Suspect – 1973, Houdini and Doyle, The Increasingly Poor Decisions of Todd Margaret* (3 series), *Tripped, Edge of Heaven, The Bleak Old Shop of Stuff, Big Bad World, Way To Go, Them From That Thing, Function Room, Him and Her, White Van Man, The Inbetweeners* (3 Series - Multi-award winning including: Best Sitcom, National Television Awards 2011; Audience Award, BAFTA 2010; Best Comedy, Royal Television Society Awards, 2010; Best New Comedy, British Comedy Awards, 2008), *The Bill.*

Film includes: *Madness in the Method, Hooves of Clay, Dad's Army* (2016), *Inbetweeners 2, Keeping Rosy, Inbetweeners: The Movie, Reuniting the Rubins.*

Directing includes: *Hooves of Clay.*

CREATIVE TEAM

Writer | Danny Robins

Danny Robins is a writer and broadcaster. He grew up in Newcastle and started performing stand-up comedy in pubs around the North-East aged 16. Since then, he has created and written a host of popular comedies for radio and television.

For BBC Radio 4: *The Cold Swedish Winter* (Series 4 coming Oct 2018); *Rudy's Rare Records* (co-created with Lenny Henry); *The Museum of Everything* (with Marcus Brigstocke and Dan Tetsell); *Paperback Hell* (with Dan Tetsell) and *Danny Robins Music Therapy*. His first radio drama, *The Most Wanted Man in Sweden*, was nominated for the Writers Guild's 2018 Tinniswood Award for Best Audio Drama Script.

For Television: Danny co-created the cult BBC2 series *We Are History*, the award-winning *Young Dracula* for CBBC and BBC1's Comedy Playhouse *Monks*. He's written for a range of programmes, from sitcoms to panel shows and has written jokes for the likes of Joan Rivers, David Frost, Armando Iannucci, Dara O'Briain, Ronnie Barker, and even Basil Brush.

Danny is a Radio Academy Award-winning documentary-maker and the host of the podcast series *Haunted*. *End Of The Pier* is his second play. His first, a stage adaptation of *Rudy's Rare Records*, starring Lenny Henry, played at Birmingham Rep and Hackney Empire.

dannyrobins.com / @danny_robins

Director | Hannah Price

Hannah is Co-Artistic Director and Founder of Theatre Uncut: the winner of two Fringe First awards, a Heralds Angel award and the Spirit of the Fringe Award. She was Resident Assistant Director at the Donmar Warehouse in

2012-2013. Hannah also directs for video games, both as VO director and a performance director for MoCap and Percap.

For Park Theatre: *The Dead Monkey*

Theatre includes: *Down and Out in Paris and London Live* (Stone House); *Again* (Trafalgar Studios); *Permanence* (Tarragon Theatre, Toronto); *Escape the Scaffold* (Theatre 503 & The Other Room Theatre); *Run the Beast Down* (Marlowe Theatre / Finborough Theatre); *1984 Live* (Senate House); *Rainbow Class* (Bush Theatre / Assembly Rooms); *TEST* (Scala Theatre, Basel); *Boa* (Trafalgar Studios); *Cello/Fragile* (Yard Theatre); *Call to Prayer* (Southwark Playhouse); *Bud Take the Wheel, I Feel a Song Coming On* (Shaw Theatre and Edinburgh Festival); *That Moment* (King's Head Theatre and National Tour); *Portmanteau* (Arcola Theatre and BikeShed Theatre, Exeter); *Loving Ophelia* (Pleasance London). For Theatre Uncut, Hannah has directed: *Refugee* (Teater Grob, Copenhagen); *In Opposition* (Paines Plough Roundabout); *Knowledge is Power: Knowledge is Change* (Traverse Theatre, Edinburgh, and National Tour); *Referendum Plays* (Traverse Theatre, Edinburgh); *TU Istanbul: Power and Protest* (Dot Tiyatro, Istanbul International Theatre Festival and Traverse Theatre, Edinburgh); *TU 2013: The Rise of the Right* (The Young Vic) and *The Cuts Plays* (Southwark Playhouse, Soho Theatre, Latitude Festival and Traverse Theatre, Edinburgh).

Associate/Assistant Director work includes: *Good Canary* (Rose Theatre Kingston); *The Machine* (Manchester International Festival & Park Avenue Armory, New York); *Julius Caesar* (Donmar Warehouse & St Anne's Warehouse New York); *Berenice, Philadelphia, Here I Come!, The Physicists, Making Noise Quietly, The Recruiting Officer* (Donmar Warehouse); *Ghost Story* (Sky Arts Playhouse).

Designer | James Turner

For Park Theatre: *Toast*

Designs include: *Dan and Phil: Interactive Introverts, The Amazing Tour is Not on Fire* (World Tours); *Great Expectations* (Malvern Theatre / UK Tour); *Before The Party* (Salisbury Playhouse); *Home Truths* (Cardboard Citizens); *Educating Rita* (Hull Truck); *Toast* (Park Theatre / 59E59 / National Tour); *A Further Education, State Red* (Hampstead Theatre); *Brenda* (HighTide Festival / The Yard); *When We Were Women, buckets* (Orange Tree); *Blush* (Underbelly); *The Deep Blue Sea* (Watermill); *Cuddles* (Ovalhouse / UK Tour / 59E59); *The Father* (Trafalgar Studios 2); *Donkey Heart, Mercury Fur* (Old Red Lion / Trafalgar Studios 2); *The Hotel Plays* (Langham Hotel); *Why is the Sky Blue?, Our Ajax, I Am A Camera, Execution of Justice* (Southwark Playhouse); *MilkMilkLemonade* (Oval House); *Love and Information; Clybourne Park, In Arabia We'd All Be Kings* (RADA); *Dracula, A Midsummer Night's Dream* (LAMDA); *Thrill Me* (Charing Cross Theatre / Edinburgh Festival / UK Tour).

Work as Associate Designer includes: *A View from the Bridge* (Young Vic / Wyndham's / Goodman Theatre, Chicago); *Rome Season* (Royal Shakespeare Company); *Antigone* (Barbican).

Lighting Designer | Sally Ferguson

For Park Theatre: *Building The Wall*

Theatre credits include: *To See The Invisible* (Snape Maltings); *Richard III* (Perth Theatre); *Again* (Trafalger Studios); *Aladdin* (Watford Palace Theatre); *While We're Here* (Up In Arms); *Educating Rita* (Queen's Theatre Hornchurch); *The Two Boroughs Project* (Young Vic); *Sweet Charity* (Royal Exchange); *Jess and Joe Forever* (Orange Tree / Farnham Maltings); *We Wait In Joyful Hope, And Then Come The Nightjars, Many Moons* (Theatre503); *Shiver* (Watford Palace

Theatre); *Medea* (Platform Theatre); *The Sleeping Beauties* (Sherman Cymru); *As You Like It, Floyd Collins* (Southwark Playhouse); *Lost In Yonkers* (Watford Palace Theatre); *Hag, Microcosm, The Girl With The Iron Claws* (Soho Theatre); *Slowly* (Riverside Studios); *The Imagination Museum* (UK Tour); *Cosi Fan Tutti* (Village Underground); *The Devils Festival* (Print Room); *The Marriage of Figaro* (Wiltons Music Hall / Musique Cordial); *The Wonder! A Woman Keeps A Secret* (BAC); *Saraband* (Jermyn Street Theatre); *Trying* (Finborough Theatre); *Little Me* (Bloomsbury Theatre / NYT); *Fiddler on the Roof* (The Bridewell NYT); *Shoot / Get Treasure / Repeat & Eschara* (Northcott Exeter); *Christie in Love, African Gothic* (The White Bear); *Whisper* (The Place / Lindbury Studio, ROH); *The Edge of Words, The Drowner* (The Place).

Sound Designer | Ella Wahlström

Ella is a London-based Sound Designer and trained at Rose Bruford. She's an original sound operator of Complicite's *The Encounter*, the Co-Sound Designer of Robert Wilson and Mikhail Baryshnikov's *Letter to a Man* and the Sound Designer of *Esa-Pekka Salonen's cello concerto*.

Theatre Sound Design credits include: *Jellyfish* (The Bush); *Trying it On* (UK Tour); *This Restless State* (The Oval House); *Of Kith and Kin* (Sheffield Crucible / The Bush); *Peter Pan Goes Wrong* (London West End / National Tour); *The Life* (English Theatre Frankfurt); *The Ballad of Robin Hood, A Study in Scarlet, Klippies* and *In Lambeth* (Southwark Playhouse); *The Bunker Trilogy, The Frontier Trilogy, The Capone Trilogy* and *Sirenia* (Edinburgh Fringe / International Tour); *Chicken Dust* (Finborough Theatre); *Titus Andronicus* (Arcola); *Theatre Uncut* (Theatre Uncut, Young Vic); *The Revenger's Tragedy* and *Henry V* (Old Red Lion Theatre).

As Associate Sound Designer: *Othello* (Frantic Assembly); *JOHN* (DV8); *The Cripple of Inishmaan* (Michael Grandage Company).

Assistant Director | Denzel Westley-Sanderson

Denzel Westley-Sanderson trained in Theatre Directing at Mountview Academy of Theatre Arts in 2017. He previously gained his First Class honours degree in Theatre and Professional Practice from Coventry University. Since finishing his training Denzel went on to be the Creative Assistant on the revival of *Jesus Christ Superstar* at Regent's Park Open Air Theatre in 2017. Denzel is currently in the Resident Directors pool at the Almeida Theatre.

Directing credits include: *Tiger Mum* (Theatre 503); *Much Ado About Nothing* (Mountview); *Saturday* (Karamel Club); *The Chairs* (Custard Factory).

Stand-Up Comedy Coach | André Vincent

André describes himself as a professional show-off. He started performing at a very early age as a boy chorister, but when his voice broke he chose not to follow his grandmother into the world of opera. Instead, he decided to copy his great-grandfather by entering the variety world, turning his hand to acting, circus clowning, improvisation, street performing and eventually stand-up comedy.

His stand-up has taken him from the comedy festivals of Montreal to Melbourne, telling jokes on countless TV shows and panel games and writing silliness for every late-night British talk-show. Surprisingly, some people must like it as he has won a BAFTA, an American Independent Film Award, Time Out Comedian of the Year and also Loaded Funniest Joke of the Year, which he is probably most proud of.

Script Consultant | Kurt Barling

Kurt Barling is a Professor of Journalism at Middlesex University. He is an award-winning investigative journalist and documentary-maker who built a reputation working at the BBC from 1989 until 2015 with a USP of covering alternative narratives in the mainstream media. Kurt's interest in theatre started in 1980 when he joined the National Youth Theatre.

Kurt gained a first class degree in Languages and Politics before graduating with a Masters and PhD from the London School of Economics where he began his career as an expert in International Relations.

He worked across News and Current Affairs for 25 years from *Assignment* and *The Money Programme* to *Today* and *Newsnight*. He was the Special Correspondent for BBC London News from 2001-2014. Kurt is author of 4 books including the latest, *Darkness over Germany* published in Germany, the UK and the US. In 2015 his book *The R Word: Racism*, described by the Times as an "eloquent polemic", was released, and a revelatory book on the security services' role in sheltering Abu Hamza from scrutiny in the early noughties.

He has brought the world of professional practice directly into the curriculum at Middlesex University and has led on transforming the journalism provision into a dynamic practice-led experience making students digital savvy and newsroom ready on graduation.

Kurt's research interests include the importance of AI to the future of journalism and he sits on the advisory board of Silicon Valley start-up Knowherenews.com.

About Park Theatre

Park Theatre was founded by Artistic Director, Jez Bond and Creative Director, Melli Marie. The building opened in May 2013 and, with four West End transfers, two National Theatre transfers and ten national tours in its first five years, quickly garnered a reputation as a key player in the London theatrical scene. Park Theatre has received two Olivier nominations, won an Offie for Best New Play (*The Revlon Girl*) and won The Stage's Fringe Theatre of the Year in 2015.

Park Theatre is an inviting and accessible venue, delivering work of exceptional calibre in the heart of Finsbury Park. We work with writers, directors and designers of the highest quality to present compelling, exciting and beautifully told stories across our two intimate spaces.

Our programme encompasses a broad range of work from classics to revivals with a healthy dose of new writing, producing in-house as well as working in partnership with emerging and established producers. We strive to play our part within the UK's theatre ecology by offering mentoring, support and opportunities to artists and producers within a professional theatre-making environment.

Our Creative Learning strategy seeks to widen the number and range of people who participate in theatre, and provides opportunities for those with little or no prior contact with the arts.

In everything we do we aim to be warm and inclusive; a safe, welcoming and wonderful space in which to work, create and visit.

★★★★★ "*A five-star neighbourhood theatre.*" Independent

As a registered charity [number 1137223] with no public subsidy, we rely on the kind support of our donors and volunteers. To find out how you can get involved visit **parktheatre.co.uk**

A Message From Juliet Stevenson

Park Theatre reverberates with life thanks to over 100,000 visitors every year. Even so, ticket and café bar sales alone are not enough to cover the costs of offering everyone a warm welcome and great experience. You can help by making a yearly donation to **Park Theatre's Annual Fund.**

Your donation will help build a pot of money to cover our building maintenance and staffing costs - directly funding two key components that make Park Theatre so special.

As an Annual Fund donor, you will be included on a special thanking wall and invited to share our success at a yearly supporters celebration.

Juliet Stevenson x

Here's how you can make a donation:

Online: parktheatre.co.uk

By Phone: 020 7870 6676

In Person: at our Box Office

By Post: Annual Fund, Park Theatre, 11 Clifton Terrace, London, N4 3JP (Cheques made payable to Park Theatre)

Visit our website to find out more about what goes on behind the scenes at Park Theatre and why our Annual Fund is so important.

Shining A Spotlight On Our Producers' Circle

Park Theatre owes a huge debt of gratitude to Ian McKellen who, in July 2017, donated a week of his time, giving ten amazing performances to help us raise money for a production fund.

Ian and a passionate group of engaged donors who are committed to helping us produce plays form our Producers' Circle. Together they help us bring productions to the stage, enabling us to tell real-to-life accessible stories that resonate and reflect the world around us.

Building the Wall was our first show funded by the Producers' Circle and ran in Park200 from 2 May – 2 Jun 2018. This critically acclaimed show brought together a thought-provoking script, tight direction, a talented cast and brilliant stage and sound design to create a show that we are very proud of. Our second Producers' Circle production, *End Of The Pier* started here as a play reading in October 2017 and we are now delighted to bring to the Park200 stage.

If you would like to find out more about the Producers' Circle or other ways you can support Park Theatre, please contact **development@parktheatre.co.uk.**

Thank You

Park Theatre aims to be a theatre for the community. We welcome over 100,000 visitors each year, run a programme of creative learning and outreach projects, stage award-winning accessible performances and offer tickets at a range of nuanced prices. **In order to do this, we must raise over £300,000 a year.**

We would like to say a huge thank you to the many generous individuals who help us on our way to achieving this target and who fund all areas of our work.

Producers' Circle:
Jeremy & Vicky Bond, Katie Bradford, Eilene Davidson, Marianne Falk, Nathaniel Lalone, Claire & Scott Mackin, Nicholas Pryor, Robert Timms, Lesley Stockwell, Andrew Wilson

Major Donors:
Nicolas Angelina, Anonymous, Michael & Sheila Black, Katie Bradford, Lady Brittan, Jeremy & Vicky Bond, The Chapman Charitable Trust, Ron & Karen Jacob, Zein Mayassi, Jim Mellon, Nicholas Pryor, Lesley Stockwell, The Theatres Trust, Anthony Zaki

Annual Fund Donors:
Eilene Davidson, Linda Almond, Sue Black, Lynette & Robert Craig, Chris & Lucie Jansen, Chris & Teresa Satterthwaite. To find out more, please pick up a leaflet or visit **parktheatre.co.uk/donate-annual-fund**

Show Keepers:
Jeremy & Vicky Bond, Heraclis Economides, Nikolas Holttum, Nathaniel Lalone, Rachel Lewis, Lucy & Gordon McDonald, Jim Mellon, Ian Rogan, Alex Sweet

Stage Keepers:
Tom Bailey, Ray Barker, Inga Beale, Kate Beswick, Katie Bradford, Carolyn Bradley, Richard Chapman, Maxwell Heath, Nick Hern, Melanie Johnson, Christine Minty, Nigel Pantling, Joanne Parker, Nicholas Pryor, Jon Shipton, Robert Timms, Andrew Wilson

Light Keepers:
Linda Almond, Stefanie Alonso y Gonzalez, Antonia Benedek, Philip Best, Sue Black, Daren Burney, Lynette & Robert Craig, Simon Fuchs, Neal Goldsmith, Nigel Higgins, Stephen Lustig, Keith Mason, Diane Reay, Francesca Simon, Lesley Stockwell. To find out more about Park Keepers, please pick up a leaflet from the box office or visit **parktheatre.co.uk/keepers**

END OF THE PIER

A play

By Danny Robins

CAST (*In order of appearance*)

Michael	30s, a stand-up comedian
Bobby	60s, a former stand-up comedian
Jenna	30s, a TV executive
Mohammed	40s, a care assistant

Please note the production may feature script changes made in rehearsals.

ACT ONE

SCENE 1: A STAGE / BOBBY'S HOUSE
EVENING

The stage is split. On one side, BOBBY sits on his sofa, the light from a TV reflecting into the room. He's in his late sixties, wearing a dressing gown, pyjamas and slippers. He's eating a sandwich and drinking a beer.

On the other side of the stage, MICHAEL stands in a spotlight, by a microphone stand. He's in his thirties, wearing a stylish suit and holding the mic, doing a stand-up routine to the audience. He's warm, engaging, and likeable.

BOBBY is watching MICHAEL's routine on TV. He laughs, grudgingly at first, but less so as the material wins him over.

MICHAEL: There are some bad people in the world, right? Isis. Donald Trump. The bloke from the Go Compare Adverts. Anyone who has ever served food on a slate...

(Beat)

But you know the worst people in the whole world?

(Beat)

People who don't have milk.

(Beat)

I'm not talking about the lactose intolerant. You're ok, if a bit whiney...

I'm talking about the people who – you're at their house, they offer you a cup of tea... then they go to the fridge and say...

(*Mimes opening fridge*)

"Oh sorry. We don't seem to have any milk."

(*Beat*)

Seem?? You don't seem to!!!??? We all agree these people are the spawn of Satan, yes? Has anyone here done this? I want to see hands...

(*In response to raised hands*)

Right, out! Away with you! Having milk is your basic responsibility as a human being!

(*Then*)

And you know the next thing they'll say...

(*Friend's voice, helpful*)

"We've got lemon?"

(*Him, mock irate*)

No!!! I don't want flipping lemon! I'm British! I drive on the left, have zero ability to learn foreign languages, always lose at football and Eurovision, and drink milky tea. That is what make us Brits, right? That and being too scared to send food back in restaurants...

(*'British' voice*)

> "Raw chicken? It's fine, darling! Don't make a fuss!"

(*Then*)

> Oh, and queuing for things. Literally anything. For no apparent reason.

(*'British', mimes joining queue*)

> "What's this? A queue? I'll join it! No need to ask what they're queuing for – we're British; we queue, therefore we am. What?! It's for lemon tea!!! Get away from me, you citrusy heathens!"

(*He does a little comic run away, laughs, and then comes back.*)

> You know what else gets me? Gets my goat. Funny expression that. "You've really annoyed me! Here – have a small bearded farm animal – that'll teach you!"

(*Makes goat 'maaaah' noise, then*)

> But no, the other thing that winds me up - Men.

(*BOBBY, mid-mouthful of sandwich, looks puzzled.*)

> Men are rubbish. I know that's a sweeping statement. The guys here, your scrotal sacks are tightening in righteous indignation...

(*BOBBY gives a little look down and adjusts his legs.*)

27

But seriously, we are ridiculous. We like to think of ourselves as these heroic hunter gatherers, because we do things like... put the rubbish out.

(*Manly voice*)

"Stand back darling. I can do this!"

(*Female voice*)

"Are you sure?"

(*Manly voice, acting out this heroism*)

"Yes! It's not safe for you. There might be bandits lurking in the night; bin-bag bandits... Let me take it, and I shall lock the door too, with my mighty man keys, that I keep on my manly fob, with my Swiss Army pen knife that I don't really know how to use..."

(*Mimes opening knife and nail clippers attacking him*)

Aaah!!! Nail clippers!!!! Help!

(*Beat, laughing at himself, then*)

Men... We like to look after things. Keys. Money. TV remotes.

(*BOBBY moves his TV remote nearer.*)

It makes us feel powerful...

(*Puts on 'superhero' voice*)

"I am The Channel Changer, controller of viewing for the entire family! And lo, I decree there shall be Bargain Hunt!!"

(*Then*)

Or ladies, how many of you have had this? On holiday, you go through customs with your boyfriend or husband, and, literally as soon as you're through, you hear…

(*Manly cough, then manly voice*)

"Darling? Where do you think you're going? Passport, please! I will look after all the travel documents, for I am man and they are safer with me. I will put them in my manly travel waist-pouch. It's not a bum bag! Or a fanny pack! It's a waist-pouch! Strapped to my manly belly – from all the manly pies and beer."

(*BOBBY opens another can of beer, the noise of the ring pull feels loud. He pours the beer into his glass and takes a sip.*)

The only thing men are actually any good at is irrelevant nonsense – like knowing all the lyrics to Ice Ice Baby.

(*Hums opening bars, then raps*)

"Alight stop, collaborate and listen…"

(*Waits for the audience to continue it, laughs*)

You see? Ask us to do anything actually useful, and we panic. You know the one

29

thing I think really separates men and women? Putting a duvet cover on.

(*Beat*)

Seriously. Guys, tell me I'm not alone in finding this 'simple task' utterly baffling.

(*Acting it out*)

"So, you take that corner and that corner, and... no, hang on... that corner and that corner, and no... what about that corner? Oh, that goes to Narnia..." It's some fiendish cryptic test – like The Crystal Maze, or Ninja Warrior! Now, every time my girlfriend says to me, "Mike, I'm changing the sheets, could you just..." I'm like –

(*Makes a heartbeat sound into mic, then does interior monologue voice*)

Please woman, do not ask me to battle the fearsome duvet cover, for I know not if I shall return..."

(*Then*)

We're like gladiators wrestling to the death. I can see the lady there enjoying that image. Me, oiled up, in a leather skirt – stop it love, you'll go blind!

(*Then*)

The only way I can do it is to actually climb inside the cover, so I look like a ghost, and then pull the duvet up from within.

30

(*Mimes this, struggling*)

> Get in! Get in, you bastard! I can't see you but I will defeat you!

(*Ghost*)

> Wooooh!

(*Then, to himself*)

> Stay focused!

(*Then*)

> Hours later, and my girlfriend's like, "where's Mike?"

(*Muffled, weak voice*)

> "I'm in here. Please let me out! The duvet cover won."

(*Laughs, beat*)

> Anyway, that's enough from me. You seem like a lovely audience, and we've got a great show coming up for you...

(*BOBBY raises his remote and turns the TV off. The lights go out on MICHAEL. BOBBY gives a heavy, sad sigh. Lights down on BOBBY.*)

SCENE 2: BOBBY'S HOUSE
EARLY AFTERNOON

An open plan living room and kitchen. It hasn't been decorated in a long time and feels dated and dusty. None of the furnishings were ever stylish or good taste, but were probably once expensive. The room is cluttered; full of ornaments, piles of newspapers, golf clubs, a putting machine, and unnecessary items of furniture, including an ostentatious grandfather clock. There are framed pictures on the walls – old posters of variety shows and souvenirs and photos from Bobby's career. On a sideboard are some awards. There's a sofa, coffee table, and a comfy old armchair.

One door upstage leads to a guest bathroom. Another door, downstage leads to the hallway. MICHAEL stands, dressed in casual, trendy clothes; the polished gleam of a celebrity off-duty. He's on his phone.

MICHAEL: Awesome. Pleasure. Yeah? No probs... (*Clears throat*) "This is Mike Armstrong. Win tickets to see me live! Only on..." Shit. Sorry. Not with it today. Course...

(*Beat*)

"This is Mike Armstrong. Win tickets to see me live! Only on Coast FM."

(*Beat*)

Bit more excited? Right...

(*More 'excited'*)

"This is Mike Armstrong! Win tickets to see me live! Only on Coast FM!! – Woooh!!!"

Was the 'woooh' too much? You like the 'woooh'?

(*There's a newspaper on the sofa. He moves it, planning to sit. Underneath is a half-eaten sandwich. He grimaces.*)

Sorry? No, that's fine. What's her name?

(*He moves the sandwich onto the counter.*)

"Hi Liz in Accounts, this is Mike Armstrong wishing you a fabuloso fortieth birthday!!! Big hugs and kisses! – Not in a pervy way."

(*He sits on the sofa.*)

Nice one. Lovely. Pleasure. The duvet cover stuff? You do that? Cool.

Awesome. Cheers. Thanks. Cheers. Bye.

(*He ends the call, looks at the clock, then checks his email. He seems tense. A beat, then BOBBY's voice comes from the bathroom.*)

BOBBY: I went to the doctor the other day. I told him I was having strange dreams. "One night, I imagine I'm a wigwam, the next, I'm a teepee. What's wrong with me?" He said, "I know the problem... You're two tents.

(*A beat then MICHAEL gives a forced laugh.*)

(*The toilet flushes and BOBBY comes out, still in his dressing gown and pyjamas. He rubs his wet hands on the dressing gown.*)

BOBBY: Your turn.

MICHAEL: What?

BOBBY: Tell me a joke.

MICHAEL: I don't do jokes.

BOBBY: Well, in that case, put the bloody kettle on.

(*MICHAEL reluctantly goes into the kitchen.*)

                 I should get dressed. You look like a
                 blooming catalogue model.

MICHAEL: (*Filling the kettle*) They don't have
                 catalogues anymore.

BOBBY: What do they have?

MICHAEL: The Internet.

BOBBY: I don't use that.

(*BOBBY straightens a picture on the wall – a large photo of
Bobby and another man in tuxedos, pulling comic poses.*)

MICHAEL: Good one of Eddie.

BOBBY: Yeah.

MICHAEL: Funny bastard.

BOBBY: He was definitely both those things.

(*MICHAEL checks his phone.*)

BOBBY: Big night tonight.

MICHAEL: Guess so.

BOBBY: Nervous?

MICHAEL:	No.
BOBBY:	Drive up, did you?
MICHAEL:	Yesterday.
BOBBY:	Hotel?
MICHAEL:	Didn't want to bother you.
BOBBY:	Thoughtful.
MICHAEL:	Late night.
BOBBY:	Oh yeah?
MICHAEL:	Stag do.
BOBBY:	Whose?
MICHAEL:	Mine.
BOBBY:	Right. Fun was it?

(*MICHAEL shrugs. BOBBY clears the previous night's beer cans off the table as he talks.*)

> What this town's all about. "There's a famous seaside place called Blackpool, that's noted for fresh air and fun..."

(*Off Michael's lack of reaction*)

> Ah, you're too young. 'The Lion and Albert'. Funny poem. When I was a kid, and we came here every summer, my old man'd do it on the train. His party piece. Albert's Mum and Dad take him to the Zoo, and he annoys a lion, poking a stick in its ear, so... it eats him.

(*Quotes*)

> "His Mother said, 'Right's right, young feller;
> I think it's a shame and a sin,
> For a lion to go and eat Albert,
> And after we've paid to come in.'
>
> The manager wanted no trouble,
> He took out his purse right away,
> Saying 'How much to settle the matter?'
> And Pa said 'What do you usually pay?'"

(*Stops, contemplative*)

> It's silly... used to upset me that; little Albert being eaten and his parents just... getting on with it.

MICHAEL: Proper Northerners.

BOBBY: Yeah. Funny what you remember. Everyone'd be laughing and I'd think would anyone miss me if I was eaten by a lion?

(*BOBBY sits in the armchair.*)

MICHAEL: And did they?

BOBBY: Oh I was never eaten. Only mauled.

(*Beat*)

> Still, you know what they say... Laughter is the best medicine. I believed that. 'Til I got diabetes.

(*He picks up a newspaper and looks at it. The kettle has boiled. MICHAEL finds mugs in a cupboard.*)

36

Teabags are in the clown.

(*MICHAEL finds a clown-shaped porcelain jar. He makes a face. It's horrible.*)

So, how's the wedding plans?

(*MICHAEL takes milk from the fridge. He sniffs it before pouring.*)

MICHAEL: Jenna's doing most of it.

BOBBY: Course. She's the boss.

MICHAEL: Nah, our relationship is give and take.

BOBBY / MICHAEL: (*Simultaneous*) I give and she takes.

MICHAEL: You need some new jokes.

BOBBY: Not much point now.

(*He puts the newspaper down.*)

MICHAEL: Sugar?

BOBBY: In the pig.

(*MICHAEL finds another porcelain jar, in the shape of a pig. He rolls his eyes and places it next to the clown.*)

BOBBY: Collector's items those. You couldn't buy 'em on eBay.

MICHAEL: You couldn't sell 'em on eBay.

(*He spoons sugar into his tea. BOBBY indicates not to put any in his.*)

BOBBY: So is she…?

MICHAEL: On the train.

BOBBY: Right.

(*MICHAEL brings the teas over.*)

MICHAEL: Said I'd swing by here.

BOBBY: Ah.

MICHAEL: Meet her later.

BOBBY: Good. She hates my guts.

MICHAEL: She doesn't hate you. It's just a very strong dislike.

(*A beat. BOBBY sips his tea. MICHAEL fidgets; he doesn't sit.*)

BOBBY: Been busy then?

MICHAEL: All over the place. North East last week. Sunderland. Newcastle.

BOBBY: (*Nostalgically*) Newcastle!

MICHAEL: Terrifying. I hid in the hotel.

BOBBY: Oh yeah, quite a challenge, the Geordies. Eddie and me were booked to do a week at some club there. Seventies. Before you were born. Did the Monday night – utter chaos; people shouting out, wandering on stage, lobbing meat pies across the room. We came off and said to the fella in charge – "sorry mate, we struggled tonight", but he said, "no, you did alreet lads".

MICHAEL: Welsh was he?

BOBBY: Sod off. The Tuesday was even worse; they had a stripper on before us; utter carnage; borderline illegal. Eddie and me come off and say, "well, we really died tonight", but, the bloke says "no, no, you honestly did quite well." Wednesday was off the scale. Chairs flying through the air, folk vomiting, passing out; some half-naked tattooed giant tries to punch Eddie. We literally run off stage and say "sorry mate, we did our best", and the fella says, "lads, trust me, you were great. Thursday, Friday, Saturday – they're the tough nights."

MICHAEL: Is that true?

BOBBY: Can't remember. I've told it so many times.

(*MICHAEL's phone beeps. He flinches. BOBBY notices.*)

That her?

MICHAEL: Twitter. (*Typing as he talks*) Gone a bit crazy. With tonight. First of the new series. Theatre'll be rammed. Everyone wants to be on telly, eh? (*Looks up*) Got any paracetamol?

BOBBY: Hungover?

MICHAEL: Bit.

(*BOBBY pulls himself up and crosses to the bathroom.*)

BOBBY: But you're ok?

MICHAEL: Course.

BOBBY: (*From bathroom*) I watched it. Last series.

MICHAEL: Cool.

BOBBY: (*Returning*) I didn't say what I thought.

(*He hands the paracetamol to Michael who takes a tablet with his tea. The clock sounds the half hour.*)

I hate that clock. When I bought it, I told them, I don't want to hear it ticking. They lied. All day long, tick tock, tick tock, how long have I got?

MICHAEL: Cheer up. You're still working.

BOBBY: Only the panto now.

MICHAEL: Bet you could do it in your sleep.

BOBBY: I did once. I was in Bradford, playing the Genie, and drifted off inside the cave. Poor old Aladdin was stuck out there ten minutes, all the kids screaming, "rub it harder you daft bugger."

(*BOBBY takes a golf club and lines himself up in front of the putting machine.*)

So how many did you get then?

MICHAEL: What?

BOBBY: Viewers.

(*He putts the ball.*)

MICHAEL: Oh here we go…

40

BOBBY: What?

MICHAEL: Not as many as you used to. Happy now?

BOBBY: Don't be like that. It's not my fault we were a 'televisual phenomenon'.

(*BOBBY returns to putting.*)

MICHAEL: Do you want that on your gravestone?

BOBBY: I'm getting cremated.

MICHAEL: I'll do both.

BOBBY / MICHAEL: (*Simultaneous, an old line*) Just to make sure.

(*They both sip their tea.*)

MICHAEL: I could murder a biscuit.

BOBBY: Oh, right. They're in the…

(*He stops himself.*)

MICHAEL: What?

BOBBY: I'm not saying.

MICHAEL: Are you denying me biscuits?

BOBBY: No, but… (*Then, uncomfortably*) They're behind the bread bin. In the golliwog.

(*MICHAEL finds a golliwog porcelain jar.*)

MICHAEL: Fucking hell!

BOBBY: Oy!

MICHAEL: What the fuck?

BOBBY: I should get rid of it.

MICHAEL: Aren't these illegal?

BOBBY: Illegal? They do the jam adverts.

MICHAEL: Not any more.

BOBBY: Since when?

MICHAEL: I'm sure they're illegal... I'm going to Google it.

(*He looks it up on his phone.*)

(*Re internet search*) No. Not yet.

BOBBY: I should still get rid of it.

(*BOBBY tips some biscuits out of the jar onto a plate.*)

MICHAEL: If Jenna saw...

BOBBY: I'll get rid of it.

(*He puts the jar back in the kitchen then returns. He offers Michael the plate.*)

They're only Hob Nobs. If I'd known you were coming, I'd have got posh ones. Duchy Originals. Or what were those I had at yours? Years back? Little Italian buggers.

MICHAEL: Biscotti.

BOBBY: Biscotti. Like chewing gravel.

(*They both take a biscuit and chew in silence for a moment.*)

So…?

MICHAEL: What? Oh for Christ's sake… Four million.

BOBBY: (*Feigned disappointment*) Oh.

MICHAEL: That's good now. They were well happy, Jenna said.

BOBBY: Not twenty though.

BOBBY / MICHAEL: (*Simultaneous*) Twenty flipping million.

BOBBY: A third of the country, tuning in for us. Two ordinary lads…

MICHAEL: In shitty suits.

(*BOBBY uses the TV remote as a mic, the old entertainer coming to life.*)

BOBBY: "It's Saturday night! Please welcome your hosts, Bobby Chalk and Eddie Cheese!"

MICHAEL: Don't sing the song.

BOBBY: (*Sings*) "Well I like satin, you like leather, how did we ever get together? We're Chalk and Cheese, Chalk and Cheese. I like those, you like these, everybody knows we're…"

   (*Holds the 'mic' to Michael, who doesn't join in*) "Chalk and Cheese."

MICHAEL: "You like leather". That was weird. What was that about?

43

BOBBY: It rhymed. Back then comedy didn't have to be 'about something'. You did it cos it was funny.

MICHAEL: God, the eighties were bleak. Thatcher, Miners' Strike and you two.

BOBBY: Whatever happens in your little life, Michael, you'll never know what it feels like to be loved by that many people. Twenty million. And why were we so popular?

MICHAEL: Because there was nothing else on?

BOBBY: Because we were the voice of the working class. We gave people – the sort of everyday people who came on holiday here or Skegness or Southend – good, honest working folk, who wouldn't get unduly emotional if their son was eaten by a lion – we gave them what they wanted to hear.

MICHAEL: Impressions of Frank Bruno?

BOBBY: Jokes. Not political or clever, not blue like your lot. Just funny. And on Saturday nights for fifteen years, it lifted them out of their lives – their sometimes hard, often unfair, lives – and made them laugh. That's why we were loved. Though, course, in the end, they used it against us.

MICHAEL: Oh God. Who?

BOBBY: The establishment.

MICHAEL: MI5? CIA? The Illuminati? (*Puts on an 'evil' voice*) "We must defeat Chalk and Cheese! But oh no, they have unleashed their terrifying Jimmy Savile impression!"

(*Savile impression*) Now then, now then, ah-ah-ah...

(*Then*) Bet you've stopped doing that one?

BOBBY: You have your laugh. But why did we get cancelled? Ok, we'd gone down to eight million, but you'd bite my hand off for that. We got called in to see that fella at the BBC. Lovely young man. Comedy commissioner, like your girlfriend...

MICHAEL: Fiancée.

BOBBY: Sorry, easy to forget, not being invited to the wedding. Anyway, nice chap. Floppy-fringed university type, John Lennon specs, stripey scarf.

MICHAEL: Is that important?

BOBBY: Never trust a man who wears a scarf. What's he hiding?

MICHAEL: His neck?

BOBBY: He took us for a Thai meal. That didn't go down too well for a start...

MICHAEL: What's wrong with Thai?

BOBBY: It's indecision in food form. "Should I have Indian or Chinese? Oh I can't decide. Let's

45

'compromise' and have Thai." It's for people who sit on the fence.

MICHAEL: You're insane, but carry on.

BOBBY: Anyway, as he dipped his crab cakes into his sweet chilli sauce, this delightful young man told us our humour was divisive. Divisive! As in, it divided people.

MICHAEL: I know what it means.

BOBBY: I'd hope so. You've been to university. You have refined biscuit-buying sensibilities. Now, he had plenty of euphemisms for it. We were "too old-fashioned for a younger audience", "too broad for current tastes", but it all boiled down to one thing: Class war. See, 'Alternative' comedy...

MICHAEL: You don't always need the inverted commas.

BOBBY: That was liked by some very influential middle-class people, and we were loved by lots of very un-influential working-class people.

MICHAEL: (*Reaching for another biscuit*) May I?

BOBBY: Be my guest. If they're not too coarse for your genteel palate.

(*Beat*)

I'm a bitter old sod, I know that, but I watch comedy now and – present company excluded, because obviously you're absolutely super-duper with all your

46

hilarious 'observations' – but I think, who is this actually for? It's not the twenty million who watched our show. It's for an elite. People who need lots of adjectives to order a coffee, who don't look at prices in the supermarket. Biscotti eaters.

MICHAEL: (*Mouth full of biscuit*) Ha ha.

BOBBY: Was it John Major said we now live in a classless society? Rubbish. The working class hasn't disappeared, people just stopped listening to them.

(*MICHAEL sarcastically applauds.*)

You saying it's not true?

MICHAEL: No. The opposite. You're dead right. Nobody gives a crap about you anymore.

The Palladium, Royal Variety, selling out the Pier – your precious twenty million... You reckon anyone gives a flying fart now? Google yourself sometime.

See what comes up.

BOBBY: (*Stung*) People forget all the good stuff... They just focus in on one... mistake.

MICHAEL: Mistake?

(*A long beat as this hangs in the air.*)

(*BOBBY gets up to tidy the mugs away.*)

BOBBY: You threw me a bit. When I opened the front door. Been a while.

MICHAEL: Yeah.

(*BOBBY takes the mugs to the sink.*)

Do you still go fishing?

BOBBY: Eh?

MICHAEL: Off the pier?

BOBBY: No. I never really enjoyed it.

MICHAEL: (*Sounding disappointed*) Oh.

BOBBY: (*Backtracking*) I mean… it was just something to do together wasn't it? Your Mum thought it'd be good for you. Joining that club.

(*Then*)

What made you think of that?

(*MICHAEL shrugs.*)

You're alright though?

(*MICHAEL looks at the floor. A long beat.*)

I should get dressed.

(*He doesn't move.*)

MICHAEL: I need your help.

BOBBY: Blimey. That's a turn up. Let me guess – you want some new material for tonight? Here's one for you – blind bloke walks into a pub, picks his dog up by the tail and swings it above his head. Barman says, "What you

48

doing?" The bloke says, "Just having a look around."

MICHAEL: I've been involved in an... incident.

BOBBY: 'An incident'? What is this? CSI Blackpool?

MICHAEL: Do you want to know or are you gonna take the piss?

(*BOBBY sits.*)

An incident is something that shouldn't have happened. Something bad. Last night.

BOBBY: Oh God. Have you raped someone?

MICHAEL: No! Fucking hell! How can you even say that?

BOBBY: Sorry.

MICHAEL: Jesus! Who do you think I am?

BOBBY: Sorry. You carry on...

MICHAEL: Bloody hell. Just let me tell you, ok?

BOBBY: Ok. Sorry.

MICHAEL: And stop saying sorry.

BOBBY: Apologies.

MICHAEL: Say nothing.

BOBBY: Nothing.

MICHAEL: Fuck's sake! This isn't some routine with Eddie, this is serious.

49

(*BOBBY doesn't say anything.*)

MICHAEL: (*Restarting*) So, I...

BOBBY: (*Offering plate*) Biscuit?

MICHAEL: You were always like this! Never took anything seriously. Even when Mum...

BOBBY: Alright! Alright! Keep your hair on. Tell me.

(*A beat. MICHAEL takes a deep breath, and continues.*)

MICHAEL: There was a group of us. Ian, Chatty Matty, Darren, Big Pete. The old crowd, from sixth form. I'd arranged to meet them for a drink, but they surprised me. Said it was going to be my unofficial stag. I was thinking great, the night before my gig... But what could I do? They took me round all these grim bars on the Prom. The ones that stink of Jaegerbombs and chlamydia. Oh, and we were dressed as Smurfs.

BOBBY: Smurfs?

MICHAEL: That was part of the surprise. You know what it's like up here. All the stags and hens – they're always something – superheroes, schoolgirls... giant penises.

BOBBY: Smurfs?

MICHAEL: I know... It was full on drinking. Tequila Slammers, Sambuca, pint pint pint. Savage, pointless. The others, they're proper lads. You know me – I don't even drink normally. I like to be in control. It got to a point where

50

they were all, "let's go to a club, a casino, the strippers…" but I needed a breather, fresh air… So I snuck off, ran away from my own stag do… I went over the road, to the North Pier. I wanted to walk out over the sea, like the old days. Escape. And maybe chunder over the railings.

BOBBY: They lock it up at night.

MICHAEL: Well obviously, but I still know the code, don't I? From the fishing club.

BOBBY: Aha. (*Remembering*) One – nine – eight – two.

MICHAEL: Still the same, after all these years.

BOBBY: Security's a joke at night.

MICHAEL: No CCTV.

BOBBY: Just old Brian in his little booth. What's he gonna do? Trip people with his zimmer frame?

MICHAEL: He had the telly on, asleep. I went straight through. I was so pissed. I ran all the way down to the very end, and just stood there, looking out, into the dark.

(*Beat*)

I didn't see him at first.

BOBBY: Who?

MICHAEL: This bloke. Fishing. (*Off Bobby's lack of reaction*) Well, this is a problem, isn't it?

51

People sneaking in at night. Fishing without permission. Non-members. People who don't pay their subs; who don't stick to the quotas, the rules... Poachers. They break in, or even climb round the sides... I read about it. It's a big problem. And this guy, there was something about him... something a bit...

BOBBY: Fishy?

(*MICHAEL gives him a withering look.*)

Well couldn't he have been a member?

MICHAEL: No. Definitely not. You can tell. So I confronted him. I just asked, politely, what he was doing. And you know what? He ignored me. And I'm thinking, listen mate, I'm someone who's grown up here, fished with permission, obeyed the rules, and you – you're going to just sneak in, steal some cod – some lovely cod and ignore me? I mean, ok, I'm pissed and I'm having a go at him, but at least have some manners. But he just tells me to let go.

BOBBY: You were holding him?

MICHAEL: I... Just a hand on his shoulder. "Piss off" he says. "Piss off." And then...

(*Takes a deep breath*)

He reaches for his bag. I don't know, maybe he's going for a knife or something, it's all happening too quickly, and I'm drunk, and this... this is so completely unlike me, but...

(*Beat*)

I hit him.

(*Beat*)

It's ridiculous. There I am, drunk, in a Smurf costume, shaking with anger...

BOBBY: Blue in the face.

MICHAEL: And I hit another human being.

BOBBY: What kind of hit?

MICHAEL: What do you mean?

BOBBY: Was it a punch or a slap? Lennox Lewis or Larry Grayson?

MICHAEL: I don't know. Somewhere in the middle.

BOBBY: Leona Lewis?

MICHAEL: I don't know, I've never hit anyone before. It wasn't hard. But it's bloody stupid. People like me... We have to be extra careful. You know that. One stupid mistake...

BOBBY: Mistake?

(*A loaded beat.*)

MICHAEL: I'm embarrassed. But this guy... he just... it really winds me up – people taking. Spoiling things for others.

53

BOBBY: Did anyone see?

MICHAEL: Like who?

BOBBY: Was anyone else there?

MICHAEL: No. It was the end of the pier – it's hidden, private, dark.

BOBBY: So what are you worrying about? Two blokes, bit of argy bargy... It happens. When me and Eddie played the old clubs, we were always getting into scraps. Had a punch up with a ventriloquist once. He was giving it all that.

(*Moves hand like a dummy's mouth*)

Forget about it.

MICHAEL: I can't. I got an email this morning.

BOBBY: Who from?

MICHAEL: Him. The man on the pier.

BOBBY: An email? Is that what people do now? "Take that you bugger, and let's do coffee next week."

MICHAEL: He must have recognised me. He emailed through my website. Said he was thinking of going to the police.

BOBBY: 'Thinking'? He wants money.

MICHAEL: He didn't ask for that.

BOBBY: It's obvious. I was blackmailed once. This fella called, said "we've kidnapped your wife. Give us ten grand or we'll send her back."

MICHAEL: Oh piss off. Piss right off.

BOBBY: Calm down... Does Jenna know?

MICHAEL: Are you kidding? To her a fight is not being allowed to take four guests into the Groucho Club, or sending back a steak at The Ivy... I don't want to worry her.

(*Beat*)

She's pregnant.

BOBBY: (*Beat, stunned but pleased*) Right.

MICHAEL: Fifteen weeks. We had the scan last month. I was going to tell you obviously...

BOBBY: But that's not why you came.

(*Beat.*)

MICHAEL: I emailed him back.

BOBBY: You shouldn't have.

MICHAEL: Told him it wasn't me. He had the wrong person. That I had an alibi if he went to the police.

BOBBY: And do you?

(*MICHAEL looks at him.*)

Oh no...

MICHAEL: Say I stayed at yours.

BOBBY: You what?

MICHAEL: Say I stayed here, got back before the incident happened. If he goes to the police, it's our word against his.

BOBBY: Lie?

MICHAEL: Dad...

BOBBY: You never call me that. Don't start now. (*Beat, considering the implications*) What about the hotel?

MICHAEL: I don't check in under my name. To avoid hassle. They'll have no record of me. The other guys will back us up.

BOBBY: Got it all planned?

MICHAEL: Look, maybe I've done enough to scare him off. But just in case, I need to shut this down. You know what the police are like... If the papers get hold of it... The bigger you are, the harder you fall. Poke the lions and they will eat you.

BOBBY: I haven't seen you in six months, and you turn up to ask this?

MICHAEL: I'm asking because you know what can happen. How they twist things, magnify it, tear you apart. I'm asking because I know you don't want me to end up like...

(*He pauses.*)

56

BOBBY: Like?

MICHAEL: You.

(*The doorbell rings, loud and shrill. They both tense.*)

                Expecting someone?

BOBBY: (*Re his pyjamas*) What does it look like?

(*MICHAEL reluctantly goes into the hall and opens the door.*)

JENNA: (*O.S.*) Surprise!

(*BOBBY remembers the golliwog jar and quickly hides it before JENNA blazes into the room. She's dressed in her work outfit – expensive, stylish, relaxed but smart clothes and geometric jewellery, carrying a leather satchel and a Sainsbury's bag.*)

MICHAEL: (*Completely thrown*) I thought we said...?

JENNA: I know. (*Kisses him*) But, just be pleased to see me alive.

BOBBY: Hello Jenna.

JENNA: Bobby. Are you ill?

BOBBY: No more than usual.

MICHAEL: What's happened?

JENNA: Something truly horrific. Blackpool.

(*To Bobby*)

                I don't know how you do it. I swear the only people I've seen are geriatrics or drug addicts. It's like Trainspotting meets Cocoon.

(*She takes a phone charger from her satchel.*)

JENNA: May I?

(*She doesn't wait for an answer.*)

BOBBY: Make yourself at home. I know how traumatic it can be, crossing the Watford Gap.

JENNA: (*Plugging in*) So, I went to the hotel…

(*MICHAEL and BOBBY exchange a nervous glance.*)

(*Checking phone as she talks*) I walk up to the desk, pop my bags down, give my name to the receptionist, she checks it. In a book. Not a computer. An actual handwritten log book. Then she looks at me, and looks at my name, back at me, back at my name and then she says, "oh, you don't look like your voice" – I'd rung from the train you see. "You. Don't. Look. Like. Your. Voice." I'm thinking, "you do" – I tweeted that. But I look at her, smile and say "clearly the 'black' in 'Blackpool' is ironic." I tweeted that too. Got a lot of retweets. Still, deep breath, stay chill, rise above, check in, walk out, grab lunch… And this –

(*Takes her chewing gum out*) Do you have a bin?

BOBBY: Under the sink.

JENNA: (*Crosses to kitchen to deposit gum*) Thanks.
Wait for it – this is the true horror of the
place…

(*Emerges from kitchen dramatically*)

They don't have a Pret. There is no Pret a
Manger. I googled – the nearest one is
Liverpool. No wonder everyone looks so
miserable. How do you cope?

BOBBY: Greggs.

JENNA: So, I wander round, dodging mobility
scooters and people shooting up, looking for
literally anything that isn't chips or
Blackpool rock, then finally fall on my sword
and get a Taste the Difference couscous
salad. Hashtag desperate times. And, I
realised you were just a short walk, so…
Have you painted?

BOBBY: No.

JENNA: Tidied?

BOBBY: Not since 2008.

JENNA: Something feels different…

BOBBY: I bought a clock.

(*They all look at the clock for a moment.*)

JENNA: Such utter bullshit.

(*BOBBY and MICHAEL look at her, surprised.*)

I didn't just swing by. I knew. I knew why
you came here.

(*MICHAEL and BOBBY are horrified.*)

(*To Bobby*) So what do you think?

BOBBY: Well, I mean...

MICHAEL: Oh God.

BOBBY: We're still discussing...

JENNA: It's a lot to take in.

BOBBY: A hell of a lot.

MICHAEL: Oh bloody hell...

JENNA: It wasn't premeditated.

MICHAEL: Of course not!

BOBBY: No way!

JENNA: But I think Michael will be a great dad.

(*BOBBY and MICHAEL realise what she means, with huge
relief.*)

JENNA: (*Slightly confused*) He has... told you?

BOBBY: Yes. No. It's great. Over the moon.

MICHAEL: Well chuffed.

BOBBY: Speechless. Do you want a tea? I think we
could all use a tea!

(*BOBBY escapes into the kitchen.*)

JENNA: (*Calls after him*) Coffee, please! (*Touching bump*) Decaf, if you've got it! (*Sotto*) How did it go?

MICHAEL: (*Recovering himself*) You could have called...

JENNA: My battery died.

BOBBY: (*Calls from kitchen*) Instant ok?

JENNA: (*Calls back*) Actually, I'll have a tea! (*To Michael, low voice*) I wanted to be with you. We wanted.

(*She puts Michael's hand on her tummy.*)

                You smell of booze.

MICHAEL: Last night. (*Off her quizzical look*) Old mates. They wanted to celebrate.

MICHAEL: The wedding.   **JENNA:** The baby?

MICHAEL: Course. Both.

(*JENNA sits and starts to take her boots off.*)

JENNA: Can you believe that? "You don't look like your voice?" London, it sort of... anaesthetises you – to what the rest of the country's actually like.

MICHAEL: Pissed off.

JENNA: What?

MICHAEL: The rest of the country's pissed off.

JENNA: With what?

(*BOBBY enters with the teas.*)

BOBBY: London.

(*MICHAEL's phone plays a reminder alert.*)

MICHAEL: Balls... Got another phone interview. More local radio.

BOBBY: Do you want to go upstairs?

(*MICHAEL looks reluctant to leave them together.*)

JENNA: Don't worry, I'll ignore him and eat my couscous.

MICHAEL: Right...

(*Michael's phone rings. He turns to go.*)

BOBBY: Michael...

(*MICHAEL stops. His whole body tenses.*)

I'll do it.

(*MICHAEL gives an almost imperceptible nod.*)

JENNA: What?

(*MICHAEL answers his phone.*)

MICHAEL: (*Forced upbeat, cheerful*) Hello! Yeah, no probs.

(*He forces a smile at JENNA and exits. We hear him as he walks upstairs.*)

(*O.S.*) The duvet cover stuff? You do that? Cool. Awesome. Cheers...

(*A doors shuts upstairs and we can't hear any more. JENNA gets up.*)

JENNA: Can I use your toilet? I haven't peed since Preston.

(*BOBBY indicates where it is.*)

Thanks. You know what it's like when you're pregnant...

BOBBY: Been a while.

(*She goes into the toilet. BOBBY crosses to where he's hidden the golliwog jar. He considers throwing it in the bin, but decides to hide it somewhere else. Satisfied, he comes back to the armchair.*)

BOBBY: Tell us a joke.

JENNA: (*From inside toilet*) Pardon?

BOBBY: Whoever's in the loo has to tell a joke. Did it with Michael and his sister, when they were kids. You're only allowed out if you get a laugh.

JENNA: Bobby, I'm literally urinating. And I don't know any jokes.

BOBBY: You commission comedy.

JENNA: Trust me, there's nothing funny about that.

BOBBY: Everyone has one joke. If you were being held hostage by Islamic fundamentalists and they said we're only releasing you if you tell us a gag...

JENNA: Is that likely?

63

BOBBY:	You never know. Reminds me, did you hear about the Irish suicide bomber? He had forty-three successful missions.
JENNA:	Shit the bed. Is that your version of topical comedy?

(*Beat.*)

BOBBY:	Well?
JENNA:	(*Sighs*) Alright. (*Thinks, then*) "How many TV commissioners does it take to change a light bulb?

(*Beat*)

Sorry, this light bulb doesn't fit our channel's new demographic."

(*A beat as BOBBY thinks about it. He laughs. The toilet flushes and JENNA comes out.*)

I hate jokes. All my favourite comedies don't actually make me laugh.

BOBBY:	What kind of coffee do you like?
JENNA:	Tall double-shot almond-milk latte. Why?
BOBBY:	Just proving a theory.
JENNA:	(*Re her wet hands*) There was no towel.
BOBBY:	I'll take it up with the staff.

(*He chucks her a tea towel. She looks at it distastefully then gingerly dries her hands. As she puts it on the counter, she notices the framed picture of Eddie.*)

64

JENNA: Eddie Cheese.

BOBBY: Before he got fat.

JENNA: Do you miss him?

BOBBY: Do you care?

(*JENNA shrugs.*)

BOBBY: Every day. They say a double act's like a marriage, without the sex. So quite like my real marriage...

JENNA: Ba dum tish.

BOBBY: Eddie was... you know the difference between a comic and a comedian?

(*JENNA shakes her head.*)

BOBBY: A comedian says funny things. A comic says things funny. Dan Leno, back in the golden age of music hall, they said he could reduce an audience to fits just by raising an eyebrow.

(*Raises an eyebrow*)

              Tommy Cooper, he was a comic. Eric Morecambe. Ken Dodd. Dying breed now. Eddie was a comic. Even after they canned our Saturday night show, when we were hosting that ropey daytime quiz...

(*He points at another picture of them – on the set of a 1990s quiz show.*)

JENNA: Ask Thy Neighbour.

BOBBY: Load of rubbish, but it paid the bills. Even then, he had it. A little look or glance. Something a bit... dangerous. I miss him more than I miss Michael's mum. That's a terrible thing to say. But you're useless, one half of a double act. Like a nut without a bolt.

(*JENNA takes out her couscous salad. Her phone rings. She looks at the caller ID.*)

JENNA: Oh go away.

(*She silences it.*)

BOBBY: Problem?

(*JENNA opens her salad.*)

JENNA: BBC Lawyer. He tried to call me on the train. They've got 'an issue' with one of Michael's gags. About that footballer. The thick one who got caught cheating on his wife. A 'three in a bed romp'. Ever had a romp?

BOBBY: Not that I remember.

(*JENNA starts to eat.*)

JENNA: Such a tabloid word. Like 'love rat' or 'pal'. Who has 'pals'?

BOBBY: Not me.

JENNA: The guy deserves everything. Sleazy romping bastard.

BOBBY: What about his wife?

JENNA: Pardon?

BOBBY: Does she deserve it? Being humiliated in public?

JENNA: Oh Bobby, please...

BOBBY: If I wanted to sum up modern comedy in one word, you know what I'd use? Cruel.

JENNA: (*Almost choking on her couscous*) What?!! And you weren't?

BOBBY: No. What we did was banter. Light -hearted, good humoured...

(*JENNA gives a disbelieving laugh.*)

                  Ok, we took the mickey, but we didn't set out to hurt. Not like Michael's lot. 'Alternative' comedy.

JENNA: It's so boring when you do the inverted commas.

BOBBY: Picking on people. Celebrities usually.

JENNA: You just have to ask yourself – are you punching up or punching down? Celebrities are the establishment. They can take it.

BOBBY: That Amy Winehouse lass... was it alright to make a joke of her? Every time I switched on the telly there was witty young men queuing up to laugh at how off her head she was. Doesn't seem so funny now. Don't get me wrong, a bit of mickey-taking, fine,

67

that's what comedy's always been about. But not bullying. Victimisation.

JENNA: All comedy needs victims. Even the most basic gag – somebody stepping on a rake or slipping on a banana skin… someone always gets hurt. We laugh because we're glad it's not us.

(*A beat. She eats in silence, looking at her phone.*)

BOBBY: Nice, about the baby.

JENNA: I'll be a fat bride. Sounds like one of your jokes. "She was so big they needed two aisles."

BOBBY: Ba dum tish. And Michael's doing well.

JENNA: We're excited about the new series. The last one was a hit.

BOBBY: Four million.

JENNA: Yes.

BOBBY: All thanks to you.

JENNA: There's no nepotism. People love him.

BOBBY: Well, of course. He's very… observational.

JENNA: I know tonight means a lot. Being back here.

BOBBY: Yeah right… Can't do enough to distance himself from me, these days. Not many even know he's my son. Heard he took it off his 'Wikipedia'.

JENNA: That wasn't him. It was his agent.

BOBBY: Didn't invite me to your wedding.

JENNA: That wasn't him. It was me.

(*A beat. BOBBY picks up MICHAEL's tea.*)

BOBBY: Gone cold.

JENNA: Maybe just try and be proud of him.

BOBBY: Oh I am. Proud. And jealous. Watching him... it's not easy.

JENNA: (*Uncomfortable*) Bobby...

BOBBY: You don't know what it's like – to have it all taken away from you. You spend thirty years building a career, think you have respect, friends, then in a few days it's all gone. Like you've got leprosy.

JENNA: What do you want, Bobby? A hug?

BOBBY: I'm not asking for pity. I took my punishment. But, for Christ's sake... A joke. That's enough to crucify someone is it? I worked with guys who shagged around, hit their wives, took drugs, drove pissed – they were forgiven. But me and Eddie... One joke. We didn't say it on telly. It was a gig. Macclesfield. You don't expect a Guardian journalist in flipping Macclesfield. Lurking, hoping to catch you out.

(*Beat, off her look*)

                  I am not a racist. You know that.

(She holds his gaze)

     I know. In here.

(He thumps his chest.)

JENNA: Sorry Bobby, you don't get to decide.

BOBBY: I had Pakistani neighbours. I gigged with Jamaican comics...

JENNA: And what did they think of it?

BOBBY: *(Awkwardly)* I didn't tell it to them.

(Then)

     It was just a joke. It didn't hurt anyone, kill anyone. Except maybe Eddie. *(Nods to the picture)* He was determined we wouldn't apologise.

JENNA: Why?

BOBBY: Said it was another example of the class war. We were being punished for using the language of the working man.

JENNA: Oh Bobby! That's such crap!

BOBBY: Look, I'm not saying what we said was ok. That word, I'd never repeat it now.

JENNA: If you did, I wouldn't be sitting here.

BOBBY: But, you and Michael, you've got your standards, standards that exist in your chip-avoiding, Ivory Towers world, lived between

	Pret a Manger and your pilates class. Things were different when we started out...
JENNA:	Yeah? We didn't use to have flushing toilets. That doesn't mean you still shit in a pot.
BOBBY:	Before political correctness came in, coloured people...
JENNA:	Please don't say coloured! Unless you're talking about the Tellytubbies.
BOBBY:	Sorry. Black people. And Asian people... They... I mean, you... well...
JENNA:	Go on...
BOBBY:	I probably shouldn't...
JENNA:	Say it.
BOBBY:	You didn't get offended in the same way.
JENNA:	We did. Just nobody listened.

(*A beat as she eats in silence.*)

BOBBY:	How's the salad?
JENNA:	Bland.

(*She pushes the salad away.*)

(*Calm but firm*) You make me so angry, Bobby. You know why? Because you're not a cunt. I would love you to be one, so I could just switch you off. But, really inconveniently, I quite like you.

BOBBY:	You'll make me blush.

71

JENNA:	But Jesus you are full of deluded shit. You talk to me like it all got lost in translation. But I went to see you once.
BOBBY:	(*Surprised*) Never!
JENNA:	Early 90s. I was eight.
BOBBY:	Strewth. Where?
JENNA:	Margate.
BOBBY:	Blimey.
JENNA:	My Gran liked you. My Dad's Mum.
BOBBY:	Was she...?
JENNA:	White? Yes. You'd have liked her. She read the Daily Mail and refused to buy anything Japanese. She took us all for a treat – 'Chalk and Cheese's Summer Spectacular'. I remember the theatre was full of people just... howling. Grown men, laughing so hard it sounded like they were crying. I sat next to my Mum and when I looked up at her face, I realised. They were laughing at us.

(*Beat*)

How dare you say your jokes weren't cruel. Every single one was like a punch. 'Blacks' were lazy thieves, Indians stank of curry, Jews were greedy, and women were either fat, slags, fat slags or joyless frigid shrews – and they definitely couldn't drive.

BOBBY: It was just…

JENNA: Banter.

(*Then*)

You know the worst thing about that day?
The look on my Mum's face. It wasn't anger,
it was humiliation. She was an academic.
This highly intelligent, career woman. And
being black, it was the one thing she couldn't
control. People joking about her hair, her
lips, how she didn't need sun-tan cream, and
if she smiled you could find her in the dark.
Years and years of 'banter', of being missed
off staff photos, passed over for promotions.
It just… ate her up.

(*Then*)

I cheered when they cancelled your TV
show. Cheered. It was like the Berlin Wall
coming down.

BOBBY: I'm sorry.

JENNA: No, I'm sorry. This conversation never ends
well. When Michael comes back, we should
go.

(*JENNA puts the rubbish from her salad into the Sainsbury's bag.*)

BOBBY: It's funny, I used to dream of people
remembering my jokes. Now I just wish
they'd forget.

73

(*JENNA goes into the kitchen to put the bag in the bin. She stands there a beat, lost in thought, then comes out.*)

JENNA: In the end, what did finally make you say sorry?

(*A beat.*)

BOBBY: Something happened. To Michael. At school.

JENNA: What?

BOBBY: You wouldn't know it now – what he's become – but he was a shy lad. Serious, spotty little thing. We worried about him, his Mum and me, that he might get picked on.

(*Beat*)

We got a call he was at the hospital. His face... It was all bruised... And his teeth... His Mum couldn't stop crying.

JENNA: Jesus. Who did it?

BOBBY: He wouldn't say. School didn't know.

JENNA: But you did?

BOBBY: We were in London then. Lived near the Beeb, cos of my filming schedule. His Mum wanted to put him in a private school, but I said no, didn't want him growing up posh. So he went to a comprehensive. Very... mixed. Apparently there was a lot of anger...

JENNA: About what you said?

74

BOBBY: The way the media portrayed it.

JENNA: So people took it out on him?

BOBBY: He never said that. He wouldn't talk to anyone. Not his mum, or his sister. Anyway, that was enough. I said to Eddie, it's not our fault, it's the press, but we need to apologise. I thought he'd back me.

(*Beat, sighs*)

He was a stubborn bastard Eddie. And he was ill by then. I did it by myself, the full circuit. Made that Channel Four documentary where I had to go and meet those campaigners; sit and listen to them call me racist to my face. Last time I was on telly. Now it's the first thing that comes up on Youtube. Three decades of making people laugh, and it boils down to a two minute clip of some fella telling me I'm scum.

(*Stops, overcome for a moment*)

The whole time, I thought, if I can get through this, things will go back to how they were – with the work, the fans... Michael. Except it never did.

(*Beat*)

So I moved us up here; only place that'd have me. Michael was fifteen. Took a while, but he seemed to settle... Sea air and all that. He was different though. With me.

(*Beat, sighs*)

> I did the summer seasons and the pantos. Exile. And I kept on saying sorry. I've never stopped.

JENNA: All comedy needs victims, Bobby. It was just your turn.

(*JENNA's phone rings. She looks at it.*)

> (*Sighs, steeling herself*) Come on then. (*Answers*) Hello Ian.

(*She put her boots back on as she talks.*)

> Yes, I got your message. No! Michael absolutely doesn't say the guy raped someone. He says he looks "a bit rapey".

(*Beat*)

> Well, we're not saying he's done it, just that he looks like he might…

(*We hear MICHAEL coming downstairs.*)

> Of course it's justified. It's satirical. It's funny…

(*MICHAEL enters the room.*)

> (*Into phone*) Hang on a minute… (*To Michael, sotto*) Let's go back to the hotel.

(*MICHAEL looks very serious, shaken even.*)

MICHAEL: You go.

JENNA: But I thought…

(*Into phone*)

A minute, Ian!

(*To Michael*)

Are you ok?

MICHAEL: I'll see you at the theatre.

JENNA: You shouldn't have gone out last night. Come and rest…

(*She reaches for him.*)

MICHAEL: (*Forcefully, moving away*) No! (*Recovering himself*) I need to… prepare.

JENNA: (*Trying not to look hurt*) Right.

(Collecting her things together, trying to make light of it) Bye Bobby.

(*BOBBY nods to her. She puts her charger into the satchel, then:*)

Nearly forgot. I got you this.

(*She pulls a stick of Blackpool rock out of her bag and gives it to MICHAEL.*)

Read the inside.

MICHAEL: (*Reads*) "I heart Daddy."

JENNA: Be funny tonight. (*She puts his hand on her tummy*) We love you.

(*Into phone*)

Not you Ian!

(*Turns to go*)

What? No, 'a bit rapey' isn't slander. It's 'vulgar abuse'.

(*As she exits*)

No, of course I wouldn't like someone to say it to me! That's why I don't have romps!

(*We hear the front door close. MICHAEL stands, frozen, for a long beat.*)

BOBBY: What's wrong? Police been in touch?

(*MICHAEL shakes his head.*)

If they call, I said I'll do it, right? I don't want any unpleasantness, not with her expecting...

MICHAEL: (*Quietly*) There's no point.

BOBBY: What?

MICHAEL: Lying.

BOBBY: It's fine.

MICHAEL: (*Snaps*) I said there's no point now!

BOBBY: Why?

MICHAEL: He's got a video. The victim.

BOBBY: 'Victim'?

MICHAEL: (*Reeling, winded*) The man on the pier. He's got a video – of the incident... There was someone else there.

BOBBY: Who?

MICHAEL: I don't know. Some friend?

BOBBY: But you said...

MICHAEL: (*Panicky, almost beside himself*) I didn't see him! I couldn't, in the dark... (*Trails off*) He's sent it to me.

(*He holds up his phone. He is shaking, almost unsteady on his feet.*)

BOBBY: Michael, it's probably funny. You as a Smurf, going off on one about fishing rights... People'll laugh. Let me see it.

MICHAEL: No! I need to... Be first...

(*MICHAEL sits at the table and watches the video, without sound. Then, he puts his phone down, gets up and walks quickly into the toilet.*)

BOBBY: Michael?

(*MICHAEL runs the water and splashes it onto his face. He's breathing deeply, panicky, out of breath. BOBBY walks over to the table.*)

MICHAEL: (*From inside toilet*) Don't look at it. (*The word comes out strangulated and odd-sounding*) Dad...

(*BOBBY ignores him and picks up the phone. He takes a moment to work out how to make the video play and then watches.*)

(*He looks shocked. He adjusts the volume so he can hear the audio.*)

(*We hear Michael, frantic, furious, shout, "you fucking Paki! You stealing immigrant black piece of shit." Then a punch and a man cries out in pain and fear.*)

(*MICHAEL comes out of the toilet. BOBBY looks at him, shock etched on his face.*)

BOBBY: Jesus, Michael. Mike? Is that you?

(*MICHAEL nods, ashen-faced, close to tears.*)

(*Stunned*) What now?

MICHAEL: I have to meet him.

(*BOBBY'S clock chimes loudly, shocking them both.*)

(*Lights down.*)

END OF ACT ONE

INTERVAL

80

ACT TWO

SCENE 3: MICHAEL'S DRESSING ROOM
LATE AFTERNOON

Michael's dressing room is spacious. There's a sofa with a coffee table in front of it and a well-stocked fridge containing bottled beers, white wine and soft drinks.

There's a mirror and a dressing table, with two chairs in front of it, and a TV in one corner.

Food is set out on the coffee table – Michael's 'rider' – fruit, crisps, biscuits, red wine, gin, vodka, tonic, cans of Coke and a bag of lemons. On the dressing table is a kettle, teabags and mugs.

There's a big poster of Michael on the wall, advertising tonight's TV recording. Near it, hanging from a clothes rail, are his stage suit and shirt.

There are two doors upstage. One leads to a corridor, and the other to a toilet and shower room.

MICHAEL is pacing. BOBBY is sitting on the sofa, now dressed in an old golfing jumper, crumpled shirt and well-worn trousers. He's holding a bottle of beer. Both of them are on edge.

A Tannoy sounds.

TANNOY: (*O.S.*) Mr Armstrong, this is your half hour call. You have thirty five minutes.

BOBBY: I thought he'd be here by now. Cutting it a bit fine, aren't you?

(*He takes a swig of beer. MICHAEL looks at him, disapprovingly.*)

MICHAEL: He's coming from work.

81

BOBBY: Risky, bringing him here.

MICHAEL: He didn't give me a choice.

(*Then*)

You don't have to stay.

BOBBY: Has he asked for money?

MICHAEL: No.

BOBBY: How much will you give him?

MICHAEL: I don't know.

BOBBY: Five thousand? Ten? Twenty?

MICHAEL: I don't know. I'll Google it, shall I?

(*He slumps onto the sofa despondently.*)

If anyone sees that video, I'm finished. Over.

BOBBY: Has he shown it to anyone?

MICHAEL: I don't know.

BOBBY: The police?

MICHAEL: I DON'T KNOW!

(*MICHAEL's phone, which is sitting on the coffee table, beeps.*)

(*They both jump, then look over at it, frozen with tension. MICHAEL reaches for it.*)

Twitter.

(*They let out a breath, a release of tension.*)

BOBBY: Jesus Christ, Michael. Where did it come from? Those words…

(*A hushed tone*) 'Black', 'Immigrant', the… 'P-word'… What was he?

MICHAEL: I don't know! I didn't stop and ask, "How would you define your ethnicity?"

BOBBY: Well, you certainly covered all your bases!

MICHAEL: Jesus!!

BOBBY: I'm trying to understand…

MICHAEL: You can't. I don't.

BOBBY: Is it because you were drunk? We all say things we don't mean when we've had a few. I once told your Mum I loved her.

MICHAEL: Are you still doing material? You're pathological.

(*Puts his head in his hands*)

Watching that video… It doesn't feel like me. I wouldn't talk like that.

BOBBY: Course not. You're with Jenna. We know you're not…

(*MICHAEL looks up sharply.*)

(*Not wanting to say 'racist'*) Racialist.

MICHAEL: You know only racists say 'racialist'? They think it somehow takes the sting off. Like saying, "I'm not a paedophile, I'm a pederast."

BOBBY: Not funny. Paedophilia is unforgiveable.

MICHAEL: And racism? They forgave you, did they?

BOBBY: I told jokes, Michael. Some of them... I'm not proud of now. But they were only jokes. I never hated anyone, or tried to hurt them. Anything I said... it was just to get laughs.

MICHAEL: Oh yeah, it was only ever about the laughs in our house.

(*He takes down his stage suit and starts to get changed.*)

BOBBY: What does that mean?

MICHAEL: Nothing. Hilarious, wasn't it? Wall to wall jokes. Either we were stuck in the toilet trying to think of them or... we actually were one.

BOBBY: You what?

MICHAEL: "My wife", "My son", "My daughter". Punchlines to your gags.

BOBBY: It was done lovingly.

MICHAEL: (*Bobby voice*) "My wife's so fat, her buttocks are in different postcodes."

BOBBY: It was a joke! Your Mum knew that.

MICHAEL: She had an eating disorder!

BOBBY: No she didn't! Michael... You're...

84

Christ... There was a phase when she was out of sorts... but... the jokes, they weren't about her. You create a character, a stereotype...

MICHAEL: (*Bobby voice*) "My son, he's got so many spots, blind people can read his face."

BOBBY: You didn't take that personally, did you?

MICHAEL: No, I was too busy being bullied for my acne. Oh, and what about this? (*Bobby voice*) "My daughter, she's a right one. Her boyfriend went to the chemists the other day to buy condoms, the shop assistant said, do you want a bag? He said no –

BOBBY / MICHAEL: (*Simultaneous*) "She's not that ugly."

MICHAEL: Bet she loved that, Karen. Probably pissed herself while she was sitting upstairs self-harming.

BOBBY: You know how it is... You've got to get the laughs.

MICHAEL: Oh you did that. Going to watch you and Eddie – it was like somebody had pumped gas into the room. People in hysterics. It's what made me want to do it. That power you had.

BOBBY: You make it sound like voodoo.

MICHAEL: Ooh, bit un-PC. But it kind of is. Cos it goes beyond just laughter. I saw the look in Mum's eyes when she sat watching you. Her face laughing but her eyes sad. A joke can make people feel things: happy, sad, small, ugly, fat... black.

BOBBY: This isn't about me.

MICHAEL: No?

(*Beat*)

Here's one for you... Funny story... One day, when I was fifteen, I arrive at the school gates, and there's this group of Asian kids blocking my way...

BOBBY: Don't. I've never forgiven myself.

MICHAEL: The leader – Imran, he's called – big fella, sporty...

BOBBY: Please, Michael...

MICHAEL: He's heard all about your joke. How did it go again?

BOBBY: (*Horrified*) Stop it!

(*A beat. MICHAEL holds BOBBY's gaze.*)

(*Shaken*) I don't understand you right now.

MICHAEL: That makes two of us. Racism is based on ignorance or fear, right?

BOBBY: Yes! My generation, we didn't learn how to speak about people different to us. Where I

86

grew up, I never met black people. You're not like that.

MICHAEL: No. But when I was frightened... I reached for it.

BOBBY: You didn't mean it!

MICHAEL: That's the awful thing – in that moment, I did. I was angry, I wanted to hurt him and those words... they gave me... power.

BOBBY: (*Shocked*) Michael...

(*MICHAEL's phone beeps. They both tense. MICHAEL picks it up gingerly.*)

MICHAEL: Jenna. Still arguing with that lawyer.

BOBBY: Oh God. What if she comes here?

MICHAEL: She won't. I told her you and me were bonding.

BOBBY: Oh, we're bloody doing that, aren't we? Bloody lovely this is. Nearly giving me a heart attack.

(*Takes a swig of beer, horrified*)

What would she say if she saw that video?

MICHAEL: She'd be appalled. You know she's on the Diversity Board at the Beeb?

BOBBY: Bloody Nora! If the papers...

(*Then*)

Are you laughing?

MICHAEL: No… It's just, they have these meetings, and Jenna's the only non-white person there. They brought her in to make the diversity board more diverse.

BOBBY: This isn't funny.

MICHAEL: I know.

(*Puts his head in his hands*)

Bloody hell… I go and visit her, at work. I take her lunch.

BOBBY: Pret a Manger?

MICHAEL: Course. When you used to take me there as a kid, it was all wood-panelled, right? Now everything's glass. She has an enormous glass-walled office. This transparent temple of diversity. And she sits in it, so… certain.

BOBBY: Of what?

MICHAEL: That the good guys won. You and Eddie were the nasty ogre…

BOBBY: Charming.

MICHAEL: And we defeated you, to live in this utopia of love and understanding, and sanctimonious Facebook posts – "Trump's a dick!" The world is saved! And I got forty-three likes!" But, what if we're not actually less racist, we're just more scared? Scared to say what we secretly think, scared to even think it?

BOBBY: You're walking into deep water here, son.

(*MICHAEL crosses to the door, opens it to make sure there's nobody outside, then closes it.*)

MICHAEL: This is what I think... Your generation had signs in the windows saying "No Irish, no blacks". Maybe we just have different words for it. Private members' club, farmers' market, Waitrose... It all still means keep me as far away as fucking possible from people who aren't like me. We live in a 'nice area'. Know what that means? Jenna barely sees any other black people. 'Gentrification' – the polite middle-class form of ethnic cleansing. Price out all the black and Asian families, do up the houses and sell 'em for a fortune to nice white people expecting babies. Cunts like me.

BOBBY: Don't use that word. Even if it's true.

MICHAEL: At the weekends, we meet our mates and chat, about how we bake cakes for Calais, send coats to Syria, and how Max and Sophie are totally cool with their neighbour wearing a burka - 'cos it's her choice'. We're all best mates with our Polish builder, Albanian cleaner, and the Nigerian bloke from Ocado, who we'd never dare impersonate the voice of! Though, sometimes, it's a Welsh bloke – (*Welsh*) And, weirdly, it's fine to do his voice, boyo.

(*Then*)

89

It's like we're all constantly sitting some exam, and if you get the wrong answer, dare reveal a prejudice, you've failed.

But just recently... Oh God... I've found myself... struggling.

(*Beat.*)

BOBBY: Go on.

MICHAEL: People call me an observational comedian. But I'm not doing that. I'm not talking about what I observe.

BOBBY: You've got your amusing lines about men and women... binbags and passports...

MICHAEL: But it's fake. It's not what I see. On tour. We roll into these ghost towns... Like here.

BOBBY: Rubbish! Blackpool isn't done yet. I'm still here.

MICHAEL: Yeah. Like the last dodo. They used to queue down the pier to see you. Now, the only queues are on Dole Day. People going to the cash-points at midnight to get money for their dealers.

BOBBY: You're painting a bleak picture...

MICHAEL: You haven't seen that?

BOBBY: Course I have. But that's why people need us, isn't it? Comedy was always the working man's comfort. If you didn't laugh, you'd cry.

90

MICHAEL: No, it's too far gone. Your audience – those 'good, honest working folk' who tolerated their children being lion food – they don't want to laugh anymore, they just want to numb the pain. That's why they come to Blackpool now – two pound pints and one pound shots. To drink and throw up and piss in the street and try desperately to forget just how catastrophically shit things are.

BOBBY: Bollocks. You go along the seafront, it's alive.

MICHAEL: It's an elastoplast over a wound. Walk a few streets off the Prom and desperation hangs in the air, like poison gas. And Blackpool isn't unique; this could be Burnley or Middlesbrough or Bognor Regis or Hull. All the bits of our country that have been written off. Where the biggest industry is food banks. And then I get back home, to Jenna and our mates – at dinner parties, or on Facebook – whining about house prices, school places, hospital waiting lists and cuts... never once stopping to think about the real reason for all this mess.

BOBBY: Which is?

MICHAEL: Maybe we're full.

(*Beat*)

Maybe there's a reason why the British are so good at queuing. Cos let's be honest, we're not that great at much anymore – football,

Eurovision, EU negotiations – but we are fucking excellent at standing politely, as people push in.

BOBBY: We're a nation of immigrants. Your granddad was Irish.

MICHAEL: Bingo. And we've finally reached tipping point. Those pictures of refugees clinging on to their rafts? Open your eyes, we're clinging to the remains of our whole country. Running out of money, food and hope. But are there any comedians talking about it? No, we're too busy ranting about the important things – Go Compare ads and Game of shitting Thrones. Say anything 'right wing' and you'll never work again. 'Immigration limits'? "Taser him and send him to Butlins!!!"

BOBBY: How did you get so angry? I thought your biggest enemy in the world was a duvet.

MICHAEL: Because the joke's on us. Every two years, funny bastards like me go on telly to get you to send cash to Africa – buy them a well – and in Rotherham there are teenage girls sucking off minicab drivers for phone credit.

BOBBY: I don't recognise the world you live in.

MICHAEL: That's cos you daren't leave the house. Still in your pyjamas at lunch time, hiding. Look at you, getting pissed just to cope with being outside your living room.

(*BOBBY looks hurt.*)

92

I don't blame you – the world is a shit shit place. And I'm bringing a kid into it. Now there's a joke. My own little diversity target.

(*They both recoil with shock at this.*)

I didn't mean that. And you will never tell Jenna.

BOBBY: It's like you're two different people.

MICHAEL: Oh, I am. I'm a double act, like you and Eddie. Nice Mike and Nasty Mike. Nice Mike, he does these lovely TV-friendly routines – "aren't those self-service check-outs annoying" and "isn't it funny how people dance at weddings?"

(*Does a naff dance move*)

People love Nice Mike. He wins Comedy Awards. Does chat shows. Marries Jenna... And Nasty Mike? Well he just sits in here –

(*Taps his head*)

And broods. Like a tumour. A hate-filled tumour. And every night I go on stage, I have to cram him down, like a Jack in the Box; push the lid tight... Except lately, he's been getting louder and louder, until sometimes I can hardly concentrate, hardly hear the irrelevant dribble I'm pissing out. But, last night, on the end of the pier, drunk for the first time in years... I caught that bloke, fishing, and he just ignored me. Some... queue-jumper, who's come here to

93

our already full country, this sad hurt town, and thinks he's got some fucking right to just take... To make things shitter. And all these feelings came out. All these things I'd been bottling up for years. Like a massive angry... burp. Nasty Mike. So I screamed that stuff at him. Those words. And then... I hit him. I hit him like Imran hit me. Held him down and punched his face.

(*Michael's phone beeps. They both freeze.*)

(*MICHAEL crosses and looks at his phone.*)

It's him. He's five minutes away.

BOBBY: Oh God. I can't cope with this. I'm putting the kettle on.

(*BOBBY, agitated, goes to put the kettle on.*)

MICHAEL: Just so I know, in case this doesn't work out... What's it like?

BOBBY: Eh?

MICHAEL: That feeling – when you wake up one morning and everybody suddenly thinks you're a massive cunt?

BOBBY: Shut up. Shut up, you piece of...

MICHAEL: Say it.

BOBBY: What's it like? It's like living in hell. Like one of those old cartoons where they saw round your feet and you fall through the floor, land with a pitchfork in your bum. It

94

happens so quickly, you don't even realise at first. For years, people've seen your face in the papers and smiled, like they know you, you're almost family... And then, suddenly, the next time they see it, you're something to be spat on and forgotten, or worse still, never forgotten.

(*Beat*)

The dictionary people, they should invent a word to describe that...

MICHAEL: 'Cuntification'.

(*Beat*)

It's like a magic eye picture. Rolf Harris, loveable family entertainer, then screw your eyes up...

(*Screws up eyes*)

Evil paedo.

BOBBY: Gary Glitter...

MICHAEL: (*Screw up eyes*) Evil bald paedo.

BOBBY: Woody Allen...

MICHAEL: (*Screw up eyes*) Ooh, awkward, we still quite like his films.

BOBBY: The sad thing is, it works on you too. One day, I looked in the mirror and hated what I saw. I'd shrivelled. Like a balloon after a party.

MICHAEL: But did you have to just cave in?

BOBBY: (*Shocked and surprised*) What?

MICHAEL: Crawling on your knees, begging their forgiveness, ringing your leper's bell?

BOBBY: Yes, Michael, I did. Because I was wrong.

(*Beat*)

My shame... is that I knew. I knew I was repeating a lie. Those jokes we told, they all came from a time before I knew any black people. I told them in clubs to white people who didn't know any either. But as the years went by... I started actually meeting them. Pakistani families moved to our road. I worked with black comics. Weird that, meeting your punchlines. And I realised something. They were just like me.

MICHAEL: So?

BOBBY: That's when I should have stopped telling the jokes.

MICHAEL: Why didn't you?

BOBBY: (*Ashamed*) Because I had to get the laughs.

MICHAEL: The audience wanted it.

BOBBY: If we didn't do that stuff, folk would come and ask why not. They'd cheer when we called those people names. Like it was some brave thing. Cheer even louder when Eddie said they should all go home.

96

MICHAEL: You were just saying what they were
                 thinking, what nobody else dared to
                 anymore...

BOBBY: Eddie would go off on one, drag me along...
                 and people would laugh and laugh. And I
                 was terrified, that if we stopped, so would
                 the laughter.

(*Beat*)

                 So, I justified in my head that the black
                 people in the jokes were just fictional
                 characters, like you, your Mum and Karen.
                 They were nothing like the ones I knew in
                 real life. And I kept telling the gags. All
                 through the nineties, into the two
                 thousands... Until finally, that journalist
                 came along, filmed it and showed the world.
                 My shame. I sold my soul for laughs.

MICHAEL: You and Eddie, you were standing up for the
                 working class. That's what Jenna can never
                 understand. Sitting in her big glass bubble.
                 Sometimes we have to defend our own.

BOBBY: We? You think you're one of us? Look at
                 you. Mr Biscotti. You're a tourist. A voyeur.

(*MICHAEL is taken aback.*)

                 'Defending our own'? Is that what you were
                 doing? Punching some Asian bloke in the
                 face? What next, you going to smack your
                 black girlfriend? Will that make you feel
                 better about the world?

(*Off Michael's shocked reaction*)

> Oh, is it just the brown ones you hate? Just the Muslims? Bit more selective these days? None of that casual racism – you've really flipping thought about it.

MICHAEL: It's not about colour, it's about them coming here, wanting what we've got...

BOBBY: That Michael... that is the biggest lie of all. Cos actually, we are all in it together. Black, brown and white, we're all getting shat on by the people who look down on us. Racism is a rich man's invention. Divide and rule. The greatest trick the devil pulled was to convince us it was someone else's fault.

(*The Tannoy sounds.*)

TANNOY: Mr Armstrong, this is your fifteen minute call. Fifteen minutes.

(*There's a knock on the door. Both men freeze.*)

BOBBY: Yes?

(*MOHAMMED speaks through the door. He has an accent, but his English is clear and fluent; defiant, yet nervous.*)

MOHAMMED: I am here to see Mike Armstrong.

(*BOBBY and MICHAEL exchange a look.*)

(*MICHAEL nods.*)

BOBBY: Come in.

(*The door opens and MOHAMMED enters.*)

(*He's in his forties, with a beard and baseball cap. He's dressed in jeans, a hoodie and jacket, with a rucksack. His body language is nervous and defensive, but there's an underlying poise to the way he holds himself.*)

BOBBY: You must be…

MOHAMMED: Mohammed.

(*He takes off his cap and we can see traces of the beating he received – some bruising and small cuts on his face.*)

BOBBY: Are you alone?

MOHAMMED: Yes.

BOBBY: Brave.

(*MOHAMMED tenses at this and retreats a step towards the door.*)

                    I didn't mean… We're not going to do anything… Relax. I'm Bobby.

(*He reaches out a hand. MOHAMMED doesn't take it.*)

MOHAMMED: I know who you are.

BOBBY: You've already met Michael.

MOHAMMED: (*A quiet, steely sarcasm, despite his nervousness*) Nice to see you again.

(*Then*)

                    You dropped your hat.

(*He hands over a dirty white Smurf hat with its distinctive shape. MICHAEL takes it.*)

MICHAEL: (*Awkwardly*) Thanks.

BOBBY: Please, sit down. Michael, that kettle's just sitting there...

(*MICHAEL goes over to make the teas.*)

                    (*To Mohammed*) Sorry, do you drink tea?

MOHAMMED: (*A beat, uncertain what accepting means to the power relationship*) Yes.

(*MOHAMMED finally sits, taking off his rucksack but keeping it close. MICHAEL looks in the fridge.*)

MICHAEL: (*Realising how this sounds*) We don't seem to have any milk.

(*They both look at him, then all three look down at the bag of lemons on the coffee table – a beat laden with irony.*)

MOHAMMED: Without milk is fine.

(*MICHAEL sets the mugs on the table.*)

MICHAEL: Sorry. Have these instead...

(*He passes a packet of biscuits.*)

                    They're... (*A look to Bobby*) Italian biscuits.

(*MOHAMMED looks at them suspiciously, then takes one and offers them to BOBBY.*)

BOBBY: (*Declining*) I'm more of a Hob Nobs man.

MOHAMMED: Hob Nobs?

BOBBY: They're a traditional English delicacy.

MOHAMMED: I am familiar with them. But I prefer digestives.

(*There's a pause as they all size each other up. MOHAMMED takes a bite from his biscuit. MICHAEL fidgets.*)

BOBBY: So... we're glad you came. To give Michael a chance to sort things out.

(*He looks at Michael, willing him to speak.*)

MICHAEL: Yeah.

(*They wait for him to say more. He seems oblivious, then realises, almost a comic double take.*)

Right... Look mate, I'm really sorry. I don't know what came over me. I'd had too much to drink.

BOBBY: You know how it is...

MOHAMMED: No. I don't drink.

MICHAEL: (*Whispered*) He's a Muslim.

BOBBY: Sorry, of course! I thought you might be, with a name like...

MOHAMMED / MICHAEL: Mohammed.

BOBBY: Well, you don't like to make assumptions, do you?

(*MICHAEL and MOHAMMED look at him with disdain. A beat.*)

(*Trying to dig himself out*) Ok... Anyway, Michael wants you to know that he didn't mean any of that stuff.

MICHAEL: It was completely out of character. The colour of someone's skin, it doesn't matter to me. White, black, brown...

MOHAMMED: Blue? I remember thinking this is strange; a Smurf attacking me for being the wrong colour.

(*MICHAEL and BOBBY exchange looks – this is not going how they expected.*)

BOBBY: (*To Michael*) You want to apologise, don't you, son? Put it behind you.

MICHAEL: It wasn't personal.

MOHAMMED: For sure. It could have been any 'black bastard'.

MICHAEL: Yes... No... Look...

MOHAMMED: You called me a 'Paki'. You have no idea where I am from.

MICHAEL: Sure...

MOHAMMED: Hoovers.

MICHAEL: Pardon?

MOHAMMED: Hoover is a brand. Not all vacuum cleaners are Hoovers. Not all brown people are...

MICHAEL: Right.

(*A beat.*)

BOBBY: So where are you from? If you don't mind me asking?

MOHAMMED: Bangladesh. It's like me calling him French.

(*Deadpan*)

You froggy bastard. You stink of croissants.

MICHAEL: Look mate, I get that you're angry. It's completely justified. What can I say? But the fact you're here... no police, no lawyers... you want to sort this, right?

(*A beat then MOHAMMED nods.*)

BOBBY: (*Relieved*) Have another Biscotti.

(*Mohammed declines.*)

Don't blame you.

MICHAEL: I watched the video. Your friend...

MOHAMMED: My son. He is twelve.

MICHAEL: Shit. I'm sorry.

MOHAMMED: He was too scared to come and help. But he knew to do that.

MICHAEL: Ok. Obviously, it doesn't look good.

MOHAMMED: No. Quite bad.

MICHAEL: How did you know who I was?

MOHAMMED: Your voice.

MICHAEL: You watch my shows?

MOHAMMED: Doesn't everybody?

BOBBY: Actually, only about four million people.

(*MICHAEL shoots him a look.*)

MOHAMMED: The duvet cover stuff...

MICHAEL: You do that?

MOHAMMED: No. But it was funny. You used to make me laugh.

MICHAEL: So why didn't you take it to the Police? I mean, I'm glad you didn't... but... why?

MOHAMMED: Because, I will not be your victim.

(*Beat*)

There are other ways to sort this out.

(*BOBBY and MICHAEL visibly relax.*)

BOBBY: Course there are.

MICHAEL: And anyway, I suppose you're not totally blame-free are you?

(*BOBBY and MOHAMMED look at him.*)

Well, I mean, you were fishing on the pier, weren't you? Sneaking on there in the dark, without permission...

MOHAMMED: I see. And fishing is only for members.

MICHAEL: Exactly. And to be a member, you have to pay.

MOHAMMED: Seventy nine pounds a year.

MICHAEL: Right.

(*A beat of realisation*)

How...?

MOHAMMED: I am a member.

MICHAEL: But...

MOHAMMED: I know, but they do let brown people in. Crazy, isn't it? So, there I was with my boy, fishing peacefully at night – you see I work during the day – when we are confronted, by a drunk Smurf, who had snuck on the pier without permission... Or, sorry, are you still a member?

BOBBY: Can I say something?

(*He turns on Michael*)

You bloody... idiot. If a lion ate you, I wouldn't ask for a sodding penny. Now you listen up, you're going to sort it out with this fella. Pay him what he wants. And fucking apologise.

(*Registering Michael's shock*)

Yeah, I can swear like you. I just choose not to, because I've got some fucking manners.

(*To Mohammed*)

Sorry mate. But as far as I'm concerned, he owes you. Whatever you want, just ask.

(*MOHAMMED nods. He unzips his rucksack. BOBBY and MICHAEL tense, unsure what he's going to bring out.*)

(*MOHAMMED takes out his iPhone. It has a distinctive Union Jack case.*)

MOHAMMED: (*Re the case*) You like my case? I got it to fit in. Rule Britannia. (*Swipes to unlock phone*) Are you on Twitter, Bobby?

BOBBY: Nah, too old for that.

MOHAMMED: Ah. It is a great way to tell jokes. They fly around the world in seconds. Mike is good at it. How many followers do you have?

MICHAEL: Three hundred and fifty thousand.

MOHAMMED: Amazing. Such power. I have fourteen.

(*To Bobby*)

Let me show you. It's easy.

(*He taps the screen*)

You compose a 'Tweet'. You can paste in a web link, like here – I've put one to the video my son took...

(*BOBBY and MICHAEL recoil, realising where he's heading.*)

Then, the Twitter addresses of people I think might be interested. A comedy website, a Guardian journalist and Mike's fiancée, BBC Commissioner Jenna Hayes.

106

(*Shock washes over Michael.*)

> Hashtag – 'Racist Smurf'. Now, all I need to do is press send.

(*MOHAMMED holds his phone near Michael's face, as if it were a weapon. His thumb hovers over the send button, like a cocked trigger.*)

MICHAEL: (*Upset, trying to contain panic*) Fuck you.

BOBBY: (*To Mohammed*) Come on mate, I know he deserves it, but don't do this – ruin his career, upset his fiancée. She's pregnant.

MOHAMMED: I know.

BOBBY: How?

MOHAMMED: He put it on Twitter.

(*BOBBY looks at Michael, deeply hurt.*)

MICHAEL: (*To Mohammed*) Go on then. Do it! See how many retweets you get for having your face thumped. You shitty, woman hating, burka enforcing, cartoonist killing, aid worker beheading, Salman Rushdie bothering, bacon avoiding... fuck.

(*A horrible shocked beat. BOBBY and MOHAMMED look at him, stunned by this outburst. We see MICHAEL himself realise how extreme it was. Then, MOHAMMED reacts – suddenly jabbing his thumb, threatening to send the tweet, right in Michael's face.*)

MICHAEL: (*Panicked*) Stop!!!   **BOBBY:** Please!!!

(*MICHAEL and MOHAMMED face each other, tense, breathing heavily, a stand-off.*)

BOBBY: What if he gives you twenty grand to keep quiet?

MICHAEL: Whoa! What you doing?

BOBBY: He wants money.

MICHAEL: But you don't do it like that! You've got to haggle.

(*To Mohammed*)

Ten thousand.

MOHAMMED: No.

MICHAEL: Alright, twenty.

MOHAMMED: No.

MICHAEL: No more than twenty five.

MOHAMMED: No thank you.

MICHAEL: I'm not going to thirty.

BOBBY: He will.

MICHAEL: Alright, thirty. But that's my absolute limit... More or less.

MOHAMMED: Stop it! I do not want your money.

MICHAEL: You...

(*Beat*)

So, hold on, you're not blackmailing me?

108

MOHAMMED: No, I am.

MICHAEL: Right. I'm confused now.

BOBBY: Me too. Is this a cultural thing? In Britain, we normally ask for cash.

MOHAMMED: And in Bangladesh, we know the cruellest form of blackmail is to ask for the thing the person will miss most.

(*MOHAMMED lowers his thumb towards his phone screen; a game of brinksmanship.*)

MICHAEL: Oh for Christ's sake!

(*Caves in, almost a spasm*)

        What do you want?

(*MOHAMMED takes a moment, relishing their total attention.*)

MOHAMMED: I want you to let me perform at your TV recording tonight.

(*A stunned beat as they take this in.*)

MICHAEL: What? Are you some sort of joker?

MOHAMMED: Yes. Specifically, a stand up one.

BOBBY: Really?

MOHAMMED: I have been doing open mic gigs for a year.

BOBBY: Blimey. How'd you get into that?

MICHAEL: Jesus!

BOBBY: What?

MICHAEL: What do you want? His fucking CV? Youtube showreel?

MOHAMMED: I have always loved British comedy. Fawlty Towers, Alan Partridge, Father Ted.

MICHAEL: That's Irish actually.

MOHAMMED: Oh sorry. You all look the same to me.

BOBBY: (*Laughs, then*) He's good.

MOHAMMED: I like jokes. So I started testing some out. At work.

BOBBY: Where's that then?

MOHAMMED: An old people's home.

(*BOBBY laughs.*)

No really. I am a care assistant.

BOBBY: Do that back home, did you?

MOHAMMED: No. 'Back home' I was something else. I did not wipe old bottoms.

(*Then*)

I did my first 'gig' at the residents' social night. I ran the bingo and told jokes.

(*BOBBY laughs, enjoying this image.*)

And I got my first heckle. A little old lady at the back… "Nurse, make it stop!"

BOBBY: I've had worse than that. At least they were probably pissing themselves.

(*MOHAMMED laughs. MICHAEL makes an exasperated noise.*)

BOBBY: What?

MICHAEL: No, don't mind me, you carry on your little love-in. Fuck!

(*He crams several biscotti into his mouth, comfort eating.*)

MOHAMMED: A colleague suggested I enter a talent competition – at the Merrie England pub.

BOBBY: Strewth. That's a bear pit.

MOHAMMED: It was terrifying.

BOBBY: What happened?

MOHAMMED: I won.

BOBBY: They laughed?

MOHAMMED: Yes. Even these two skinheads on the front row. When I got up on stage, I heard them whisper, "This Paki had better be funny." Then, after the gig, they asked me for a selfie.

(*He and BOBBY laugh.*)

When the MC announced I'd won, I was so happy. I took my winner's cheque and danced down the street, onto the beach. Even though it was late, I ran into the sea; threw myself in the cold water with all my clothes on, whooping, "I won! I won!"

BOBBY: Good on you son.

111

MOHAMMED: Unfortunately, I still had the cheque in my pocket... But that night... If you can make people laugh, it is harder for them to hate you.

(*Beat, then to Michael*)

So now, I want to be on TV. Just like you.

MICHAEL: You're mental mate. You can't just walk onto a primetime comedy show.

MOHAMMED: I understand. Sorry for asking. I will just send the tweet.

(*He reaches for the button.*)

MICHAEL: (*Panicked*) No!

(*The Tannoy sounds.*)

TANNOY: Mr Armstrong, this is your five minute call. Five minutes.

MICHAEL: (*Agonised*) Why can't you just ask for money?

MOHAMMED: (*Impassioned*) Because I want you to watch your audience enjoying the very thing you hate – a brown – skinned immigrant, coming over here, taking your laughs. I want you to see me being funnier than you, on your own stage. I want that to hurt; to feel humiliating. I want to take the thing you will miss most. Your power.

(*Then*)

So, what's it going to be?

112

(*He waggles his thumb over the phone.*)

(*MICHAEL crumples, his resistance over.*)

(*Lights down.*)

SCENE 4: THEATRE STAGE / MICHAEL'S DRESSING ROOM
LATER

The stage is split. On one side, the theatre stage is set for the filming of 'Mike Armstrong's Comedy Getaway'. MICHAEL is lit by a spot, standing by a microphone stand, holding the mic, doing his stand-up routine.

On the other side, BOBBY and JENNA sit in the dressing room, drinking and watching the live feed from the recording on the TV.

MICHAEL: Another thing that gets my goat...

(*Makes goat noise*)

> Those serving suggestions they stick on food packets. You know – like on cornflakes – 'Serving suggestion' and a little picture of cornflakes in a bowl with milk. You what? I was just about to sauté them with a few quail's eggs in a red wine jus!

(*Beat*)

> Orange juice – 'In a glass'? What is this devilry!? I'd planned to drink it from my shoe!"

(*Mimes drinking from his shoe*)

> Mmm, juicy shoe, yum yum...

(*Then*)

> We live in a mad world. A mad mad world...

(*A beat, as he loses his flow*)

> Sorry, long day... Did I tell you I'm expecting a kid? Woooh! People keep warning me about the not sleeping, the waking up screaming, the shitty knickers. And I'm like, yeah, I've already got that.

(*He looks across at Jenna, then*)

> They'll edit that out. Beauty of TV.

(*Then*)

> Right, we've just got time for one more act.

(*JENNA looks surprised and concerned.*)

> He's come all the way from Bangladesh. Please welcome... Mohammed Hasan.

(*MOHAMMED comes onto the stage. He has smartened himself up.*)

(*MICHAEL hands him the microphone, avoiding eye contact, then walks off, into the dressing room.*)

JENNA: What the hell's going on?

(*MICHAEL won't meet her eye. A long beat as MOHAMMED stands there, like a rabbit in headlights.*)

MOHAMMED: (*Uncertainly*) Hello...

(*BOBBY tenses. MICHAEL smiles with sly satisfaction at the thought this is going horribly wrong.*)

(*JENNA moves to go out on stage, but BOBBY holds her back.*)

BOBBY: (*Sotto, but forceful*) Give him a chance.

(*MOHAMMED takes a breath and we see him mentally switch into gear. He starts tentatively, but grows in confidence.*)

MOHAMMED: So, yeah, I am from Bangladesh. Of course, we're not the trendy asylum seekers. That's the Syrians. I'm so sick of them, coming over here, taking our benefits, seeking our asylum...

(*As he gets his first laugh, he relaxes. Finding his flow, we realise he is a natural stand-up, funny and warm on stage.*)

(*JENNA looks surprised. As the routine goes on, she and BOBBY laugh more and more, slowly becoming enthralled.*)

(*MICHAEL does his best to suppress any laughter, looking increasingly defeated.*)

Do we have any immigrants in tonight?

(*Waits for audience hands up*)

Yay! We found them! Quick, call the Home Office!

(*Laughs, then*)

I have been in Britain five years now. I love this country. I love the way you are always so sorry for everything. You apologise even if I am in the wrong.

(*Perfect British accent*)

"Sorry, you seem to have stepped on my foot, sorry, my fault, I really shouldn't have feet, bloody silly things"

(*To feet, shaking them, still British*)

116

"Get off! Get off me, you idiots!"

(*Then*)

I banged into a man the other day, on the train. I spilt his coffee, and he said sorry to me. I offer to buy him a new one, just ask him to watch my rucksack, and he runs off! What did I do?

(*Beat*)

Actually, I have found the perfect way to always get a seat on the train – I put an alarm clock in my rucksack – tick tick tick! People move bloody quickly! You can also say stuff like, "mmm, boy, am I looking forward to meeting all those virgins."

(*Beat*)

Seriously though, you should see your faces when someone like me gets on with a backpack. You're smiling, but your brain is going...

(*Low, into mic*)

Get off the train! The brown guy is about to explode!

(*Then*)

But then you think, "Oh God! That will look racist!" So you have this conversation in your head – would you rather look racist or dead?

117

(*To an audience member*)

Racist or dead?

(*Then, acting this out*)

Finally, you compromise and just casually move carriage – away from the blast zone! But do you warn anyone else? No! You'd rather let a whole carriage die than look racist! You ruthless politically correct bastards!!! Hands up if you've done that?

(*To anybody without hands up*)

Liars! Trust me, I'm brown and I've done it. Big beard, baseball cap – jihadi or hipster? So hard to tell... Offer him a craft beer, that's the test. "Pale ale?"

(*Jihadi cry*)

"Allahu Akbar!"

(*Makes explosion noise, then laughs*)

But you guys, you are not quite sure what to do with us immigrants. We should be more British – that's what I always hear.

(*British voice*)

"Immigrants to Britain must adapt to our way of life".

(*Then*)

Well, going to someone else's country, only eating your own food, not bothering to speak

118

the language – that sounds pretty bloody British to me!

(*Beat*)

Seriously, I don't want to be rude – I love you guys! – but you have this bad habit of just turning up, partitioning countries and running away. Palestine, Ireland, us...

(*Then*)

"Hey India! Meet Pakistan! You guys play nicely! Bye!"

(*Then*)

You are like geographic serial-killers. Everyone you meet ends up in bits. And now maybe the Scottish want to do it back to you – partition the UK! Can you can imagine the negotiations?

(*Scottish*) "You can have the debt and Brexit. But we're keeping Andy Murray!"

(*Then*)

But, Bangladesh – I should go back to that – as the UK Border Agency once said. When I was a kid, in the Seventies, we had a war with Pakistan. It's ok, you've never heard of it. I mean, you started it, one million people died, but it was a 'brown war'. It got knocked off the News by The Wombles getting to Number One.

(*Then*)

We were lucky – my parents had some money, so we escaped here, to the UK – to Leeds – I said we had some money...

(*Then*)

We tried so hard to integrate, to learn your customs. "Yorkshire pudding"? That is not a pudding! It is bread that has had a stroke!

(*Then*)

I spent most of my time being chased by skinheads wanting to 'Paki-bash' me.

I would be explaining...

(*Mimes running*)

"Guys, we have lots in common! I am from Bangladesh! We are currently bashing Pakis too!"

(*Beat*)

You know the British thing I most envied? Christmas! Oh my Gosh! You are so lucky! All the kids at school would say...

(*Yorkshire accent*)

"Ay up... Ay up, you Muslims, what's your big celebration?"

(*Him*)

"Ramadan".

(*Yorkshire*)

"Oh! What do you do then?"

(*Him*)

"Don't eat for a really long time."

(*Then*)

It sucks, man! Muslims would be so good at Christmas. Santa – beard, hides in a grotto for most of the year, big bag full of 'surprises' – he's one of us! Imam Claus.

(*Beat*)

"Ay up!" How's my Yorkshire accent? It's not fair, is it? I can do white guy voices but as soon as you do a brown guy...

(*Peter Sellers-style 'Asian' accent*)

"Thank you very much. Goodness Gracious me..."

(*Makes a klaxon noise*)

"Racist alert! Back away from the accent."

(*Holds mic to audience member*)

Go on. Have a go. It's fine. I won't judge. Go on, just say...

(*Heavily accented*)

"Chicken Tikka Massala."

(*Snatches mic back*)

What are you doing???! You racist!!!

(Laughs, then)

> When I got a bit older, my parents moved us
> back to Bangladesh. They missed it – the
> floods, cyclones, poverty, corruption,
> religious fundamentalism... I went to uni,
> and became a journalist. Which was great.
> Until I had kids. Cos something changes,
> right?

(In the dressing room, MICHAEL reacts to this.)

(To audience)

> Who's a parent? Do you find yourself crying
> at stuff? Films? TV? I watched Peppa Pig
> the other day and I wept! But mainly
> because a pig is an unclean animal! Peppa is
> not halal!

(Then)

> But seriously, you care more... About what
> kind of world your kids will live in. So, I
> spoke out. About the poverty, corruption,
> religious fundamentalism. This is another
> way you're lucky! Your government sucks,
> but they don't mind you telling them!
> Imagine if Boris Johnson had the power to
> have you tortured – and I don't mean in a
> kinky boarding school way. Or having to
> read one of his books. Real torture. Beatings.
> Electric shocks. Removing fingernails.

(He holds up his hand. Some of his nails are missing.)

They told me to give up the names of the people involved in my 'dissident network'. I said, "I will never tell you, and whatever you do, don't look on Facebook."

(*Beat*)

So I had to escape. It's nice to be back. All the reassuring old stuff – Yorkshire pudding, being chased. Except now you don't call it 'Paki-bashing', because that is racist. Now, I get 'Muslim-bashed'.

(*Mimes running*)

EDL guys shouting –

(*EDL thug voice*) "Oy! you brought Sharia Law to Britain!" Sharia Law here, Sharia Law there. I'm like, who are you – Stevie Wonder?

(*Sings, to tune of 'My Cherie Amour'*)

"My Sharia Law!"

(*Mimes being hit*)

Ow! You still don't do irony!

(*Then*)

We need to have some laughs, right? Cos, there's a lot of hate around. Facebook, Twitter – people are so angry! And I get it. You're living in tough times, the country's a mess, you have to decide on a daily basis between The Chase and Pointless... life is hard. And then you face the threat of extremists trying to destroy everything you hold dear... but hey, you voted for them...

(Beat)

And all this crap, it must be somebody's fault. So you look for someone to blame it on. The EU? The Grinch? The Boogie? But immigrants just seems easier. Cos they won't answer back. Most don't even speak the bloody language!

(Beat)

But let's look at the facts, shall we? Who's really to blame? Cos I'm pretty sure the Pakistanis did not close your mines. The Romanians did not sell off your public services. The Somalis didn't introduce PFI and cripple your hospitals with debt. And the Syrians aren't opening offshore accounts to avoid paying tax. In fact, most refugees don't feel that comfortable with the word 'offshore'.

(Beat)

You are being beaten by your father and you lash out at your brother.

(Beat)

Think I split the room. Fifty two / forty-eight.

(Then)

124

Ok, here's what I don't get. You came over to us. To the Caribbean, Africa, India. For two hundred years, you took our cotton, our coal, our gold, our jewels, our soldiers, our labour, even our food... Any Churchill fans in? We love him right? He won the war. Gave us cheap car insurance... Know what else he did? In 1943, he diverted food from India and sent it to British soldiers. Three million Indians starved to death. That's half a Holocaust.

(*Beat*)

You know what lovable old Winston said?

(*Churchill impression*)

"I hate Indians. The famine was their own fault for breeding like rabbits."

(*Then*)

You didn't hear Gary Oldman say that did you?

(*Beat*)

You even took our food. And now, you don't want us? You're like:

(*Then*)

"We enjoyed screwing you, but it was nothing serious. We were just friends with benefits." And we're like, "'benefits'? Mmmm. Sounds good"

125

(*Then*)

> But if we leave, we're going to take our food
> back. Which could be a problem, because, as
> we all know, the most popular dish in the
> UK is...

(*Goes over to person he picked on earlier*)

> Say it... Do the voice. It's really ok...

(*Whispers*)

> Chicken tikka masala

(*When they say it*)

> You racist!!!

(*Then*)

> Thanks for listening. If you've enjoyed me,
> I've been Mohammed Hasan if not, I've been
> Cat Stevens. Find me on Twitter! Good
> night!

(*BOBBY AND JENNA break into applause.*)

(*MICHAEL looks down, utterly empty.*)

(*Lights down, first on Mohammed and then on Michael.*)

SCENE 5: MICHAEL'S DRESSING ROOM
AFTER THE SHOW

(*LIGHTS up on JENNA and BOBBY. They have drinks, they've just finished watching the recording.*)

JENNA: I'm appalled.

BOBBY: Really?

JENNA: Putting on another act without telling me? It completely screwed the schedule!

(*She turns to face him*)

But... he was absolutely amazing.

BOBBY: Wasn't he?

JENNA: I mean Michael was great too, he always is. Really...

BOBBY: Observational.

JENNA: But that guy... Oh my God. I had this little moment, where I realised why I've never liked jokes. It's because they're almost always based on a lie.

BOBBY: Chickens don't cross the road.

JENNA: Even Michael does it. Between you and me, he knows exactly how to put a duvet cover on.

BOBBY: (*Smiles*) Does it matter?

JENNA:	Yes. Because if you start to rebuild reality just to get laughs, where do you stop? The truth is important. And funnier.
BOBBY:	Michael didn't do that gag about the footballer.
JENNA:	No.
BOBBY:	Lawyer won then?
JENNA:	Oh no, I talked him round. I'm pretty persuasive. But then I saw a link on Twitter – an interview with the guy's wife. She's pregnant.

(*She touches her own tummy.*)

	I guess I thought about my Mum. Her face at your show. Not all jokes need to be told.
BOBBY:	She'd have been proud of you.
JENNA:	Thank you for staying out of the way tonight. Being discreet.
BOBBY:	It's always going to be like this, isn't it?

(*JENNA nods. BOBBY opens another beer.*)

	My local vicar, when I was a kid, he used to tell this story, about a fella who had the letters 'S.T' branded on his forehead. Heard that one? He's a lovely old bloke, helpful, kind, and everyone assumes it stands for 'Saint'. Turns out he used to be a Sheep Thief.

(*Then*)

People can change.

JENNA: Can you do something for me? Well, for Mum, really. Sort of like a wedding gift?

(*BOBBY nods.*)

Smash that fucking horrible golliwog jar you hide in your kitchen. And throw away the pieces.

BOBBY: Yes.

(*The door opens and MOHAMMED enters.*)

(*JENNA and BOBBY give a cheer.*)

JENNA: That was bloody brilliant! You were hilarious!

MOHAMMED: Thank you.

JENNA: You really are from Bangladesh? It wasn't just part of the act?

MOHAMMED: No.

JENNA: Brilliant. And you actually got tortured?

MOHAMMED: Yes.

JENNA: Brilliant. God, I mean... Sorry!

(*Refs Mohammed's 'Sorry' routine*)

Sorry! So British!

(*Then*)

It's just, we've been looking for someone like you for ages.

(*MICHAEL enters.*)

Genius booking, darling. Even if it was a surprise.

(*She kisses him. He flinches at her touch. She notices.*)

We should let you get changed.

(*To Mohammed*) Can I buy you a drink upstairs? Obviously not a beer!

MOHAMMED: Very thoughtful.

JENNA: What about juice?

MOHAMMED: I have nothing against them as long as they respect Palestine.

JENNA: No, I meant... Oh you're joking. Jews. Juice... Brilliant. We should get you on 'Have I Got News For You'! We're pushing them to be more diverse.

MOHAMMED: I could wear a traditional Islamic outfit – if that helped.

JENNA: Well, that might actually be great...

MOHAMMED: Like an orange jumpsuit?

(*BOBBY laughs.*)

JENNA: (*Realising she's being spoofed*) I'll shut up.

(*To Bobby, clearly not wanting him to follow*) Bobby?

130

BOBBY: (*Re Michael*) I'll help him with his buttons.

                    (*To Mohammed*) It was a cracking set, son. Especially for a...

MOHAMMED: Paki?

BOBBY: (*Smiles*) Open spot.

MOHAMMED: Thank you.

(*MOHAMMED picks up his rucksack and looks over at MICHAEL.*)

                    (*Colder, more formal*) Thanks.

(*MICHAEL nods to him, expressionless.*)

                    (*Leans in, so only Michael can hear*) It is always easier to punch down, but he who punches up, lands the knockout blow.

(*He turns away, back to Jenna.*)

JENNA: (*To Michael*) Don't be long.

(*She touches her bump instinctively, then she and MOHAMMED exit. We hear them talking from the corridor as they walk away.*)

                    So, 'Mohammed' after the prophet, obviously...

MOHAMMED: No, actually, after my uncle...

(*BOBBY shuts the door and goes to sit next to Michael. They stay like that for a long moment, in silence.*)

BOBBY: You have to admit he was funny.

131

MICHAEL: Oh he was.

(*BOBBY looks to see if he's being sarcastic.*)

I mean it. Timing. Delivery. Funny. Funnier than me. And you know why? Cos he told his truth.

(*BOBBY drains his beer and sets it on the table.*)

BOBBY: I need a pee. Blooming diabetes. Bladder like a bust sieve.

(*He gets up to go to the toilet.*)

MICHAEL: I lost.

BOBBY: Yeah. But you saved your career. Nice Mike.

(*He goes into the toilet.*)

(*MICHAEL stands up to get changed. He notices that Mohammed's phone, with its distinctive Union Jack case, has been left on the dressing table. He picks it up, holds it, thinking.*)

(*From inside toilet*) Me and the wife, our sex life's not what it was. She said she thought we'd lost the excitement. Came home from the shops and said, "Don't treat me like your wife, treat me like your girlfriend." I said, "Ok, climb through that window." She said, "Why?" I said, "Cos my wife's just got home."

(*MICHAEL swipes Mohammed's phone, unlocking it. He finds the Tweet Mohammed wrote, thinks about it for a moment.*)

We celebrated our anniversary the other day. I took her to a Japanese restaurant.

132

>Waiter came over, I said, "I'll have some of that rice wine". He said, "Saki?" I said, "No, I really mean it."

(*MICHAEL decisively pushes a button on the screen.*)

>Still, at least I've got my health. Mate of mine went to the hospital, the Doctor said "I'm afraid it's bad news. You've only got seven days to live." "Oh no", he gasped. "It gets worse," said the Doctor. "I should have told you last week."

(*MICHAEL puts the phone back down on the table. A beat.*)

>Come on, let me out.

(*MICHAEL gives a forced laugh in the direction of the toilet, then goes to get a beer from the fridge.*)

(*The toilet flushes. BOBBY comes out.*)

MICHAEL: You're wasted on panto.

BOBBY: "Oh no I'm not…"

(*MOHAMMED's phone starts pinging.*)

>That yours?

(*MICHAEL shakes his head. BOBBY picks up the phone and sees it's Mohammed's.*)

>Oh, well, I guess he'll be back for it.

(*The phone keeps pinging. MICHAEL silences it, then starts to get changed.*)

>Busy week coming up?

MICHAEL: Might work on some new material.

BOBBY: I'd stick to what you've got.

(*MICHAEL takes a swig of beer. A long beat.*)

MICHAEL: At night, I lie next to her, looking at her tummy, that little bump growing, and I have this noise in my head. I can't stop it. It's louder than anything else.

BOBBY: I look at you, and you know who I see? Eddie.

MICHAEL: Well, he was always the funnier one.

BOBBY: Yeah, he was. Funny and nasty.

(*Beat*)

There's one time that sticks in my head. I was at his house, writing, would have been late eighties. This Asian family had moved in next to him. Must have been rich, cos Eddie was living in one of those big posh houses, opposite the Crematorium. We'd been working all morning – me typing away, Eddie talking about golf, like normal – and we needed a breather, so we went out into the garden and, next door, there were these two little Asian kids playing; running around and giggling. Not too loud, just having fun, but I could see it was bothering Eddie. He went back into the house, and at first, I thought that was it; he'd disappeared because he couldn't face being near them. He always said he could smell them through the

134

walls of his house. But then he came back out, smiling, and he had two small lollipops, that he handed over the fence to the kids. I was totally wrong-footed, and when we went back upstairs, I said to him, that was nice, what you did... And he grinned – this big, nasty, sly grin – and told me he'd smeared the lollipops around the toilet bowl first, to pick up as many germs as possible. All Eddie's piss and shit. He thought it was hilarious. Laughed more at that than anything we'd written all day.

(*Beat*)

Full of hate, he was, and dead at fifty five. A big fat angry corpse. He had a bad heart, Eddie, in more ways than one.

(*He puts a hand on Michael's shoulder, quiet, intense*)

Don't give in to it.

MICHAEL: Imran.

BOBBY: Eh?

MICHAEL: That boy at the school gates. I've never told you the reason he attacked me.

BOBBY: I guessed.

MICHAEL: No you didn't.

(*Beat*)

It was because I said it to him.

BOBBY: What?

135

MICHAEL: I told him your joke.

BOBBY: (*Like a punch to the stomach*) Jesus, Michael. Why?

MICHAEL: Because he knew you'd lost, and he was standing there, smug, looking down at me like I was nothing. "Excuse me," I said, trying to get past. And he doesn't even acknowledge me. Just turns his head, dismissively. Ignores me. And I think alright then, so I say it... The first joke I ever told in public. And just for a moment, it was like I'd punched him. He crumples, shrinks, and I can almost feel the transfer of power. And you know how it felt? Fucking fantastic. Like I'd won.

(*BOBBY sits, broken.*)

BOBBY: In the hospital... When you wouldn't say what happened... I thought you were ashamed of me. All these years, I've thought you were ashamed.

MICHAEL: I was. Ashamed that you'd apologised. That you'd given in.

(*There's a knock on the door.*)

Come in.

(*MOHAMMED enters.*)

MOHAMMED: (*In a good mood, fresh from being praised by Jenna*) Hi! Sorry! I forgot my phone.

(*MOHAMMED picks the phone up. He looks at it, seeing the Twitter mentions on the front screen. He is shocked.*)

Hang on, what…?

(*He swipes the screen and reads more.*)

(*Aghast*) Did you…?

(*He looks at Bobby and then Michael.*)

What have you done?

(*We hear the sound of JENNA screaming from some distance off – a cry of anguish.*)

BOBBY: (*Confused*) Michael?

MOHAMMED: Oh my God. The tweet. With the video. He sent the tweet!

(*We hear JENNA running toward the dressing room.*)

JENNA: (*A wail of pain as she runs*) Michael!!!

(*The door bursts open.*)

(*Through tears, out of breath*) I don't understand… The video… Is that you?

BOBBY: (*Shocked, like a punch to the stomach*) Oh no…

(*MICHAEL smirks, showing his guilt.*)

JENNA: How could you? Hit him like that? I don't understand…

MOHAMMED: You're insane, man. What about your show?

137

JENNA: (*To Mohammed*) Oh God! They won't broadcast it now...

(*Then*)

Those words... Do you really think like that? Is that what you think of... me?

(*She touches her stomach.*)

Us?

(*She goes to him and places his hand on her belly.*)

Michael, what do you think when you look at me?

(*A beat.*)

MICHAEL: You don't look like your voice.

(*JENNA reels, winded.*)

JENNA: No. How could you be so cruel?

(*MOHAMMED moves towards Michael with surprising speed and force. He raises his fist, as if about to hit him. MICHAEL flinches. MOHAMMED is holding his phone in his fist. He holds the screen towards Michael.*)

MOHAMMED: Look. See what you have done. Because of that video – I have five thousand followers! And more coming every minute. You lose. You immigrant-attacking, hate-mongering, myth-spreading, white-power fantasising, diversity-belittling, duvet-cover-avoiding, truth-ignoring... fuck.

(*MICHAEL starts to laugh.*)

JENNA: Stop it! Stop it! It's not funny!

(*BOBBY walks up to Michael and leans in, his face close to MICHAEL's ear. MICHAEL stops laughing.*)

BOBBY: Welcome to Hell.

(*Lights down.*)

END